TODAY'S WRITERS
AND THEIR WORKS

SANDRA CISNEROS

Raychel Haugrud Reiff

Cavendish
Square

New York

813.54
Rei

Published in 2014 by Cavendish Square Publishing, LLC
303 Park Avenue South, Suite 1247, New York, NY 10010
Copyright © 2014 by Cavendish Square Publishing, LLC
First Edition

Website: cavendishsq.com

This publication represents the opinions and views of the author based on his or her personal experience, knowledge, and research. The information in this book serves as a general guide only. The author and publisher have used their best efforts in preparing this book and disclaim liability rising directly or indirectly from the use and application of this book.

Pub
3/14

CPSIA Compliance Information: Batch #WS13CSQ

All websites were available and accurate when this book was sent to press.

Library of Congress Cataloging-in-Publication Data
Reiff, Raychel Haugrud. • Sandra Cisneros / Raychel Haugrud Reiff. • p. cm.—
(Today's writers and their works) • Includes bibliographical references and index.
Summary: "Explores the life, work, and themes of author Sandra Cisneros"—
Provided by publisher. • Includes filmography.
ISBN 978-1-62712-151-4 (hardcover) ISBN 978-1-62712-145-3 (paperback)
ISBN 978-1-60870-759-1 (ebook)
1. Cisneros, Sandra—Juvenile literature. I. Title. II. Series.
PS3553.I78Z83 2011 • 813'.54—dc22 • 2010042466

Art Director: Anahid Hamparian
Series Designer: Alicia Mikles • Photo research by Lindsay Aveilhe
The photographs in this book are used by permission and through the courtesy of:
Cover photo by Eric Gay/AP Photos; Ray Santisteban: p. 4; Pictorial Press Ltd/Alamy:
p. 8; Ray Santisteban: p. 11; Photograph by Diana Solis: p. 16; Damon Winter/The New
York Times/Redux: p. 23; Mel Finkelstein/NY Daily News Archive via Getty Images: p. 27;
Hillery Smith/Newscom: p. 43; Courtesy of Vintage a division of Random House, April 3,
1991: p. 48; Lebrecht Music & Arts/The Image Works: p. 54; (left to right) Christina Nieves,
Belinda Cervantes and Sandra Delgado (Mari Stratton, upper left) in Steppenwolf for Young
Adults' of The House on Mango Street by Tanya Saracho, based on the novel by Sandra
Cisneros and directed by Hallie Gordon. Photo by Peter Coombs: p. 61; (left to right)
Belinda Cervantes, Sandra Delgado and Christina Nieves in Steppenwolf for Young Adults'
of The House on Mango Street by Tanya Saracho, based on the novel by Sandra Cisneros
and directed by Hallie Gordon. Photo by Peter Coombs: p. 70; Courtesy of Vintage a division
of Random House, March 3rd 1992: p. 77; Everett Collection: p. 80; Iain Masterton/Alamy:
p. 81; Steve Skjold/Alamy: p. 87; Courtesy of Knopf, a division of Random House,
November 17, 1992: p. 92; Blend Images/Alamy: p. 98; Courtesy of Knopf, a division of
Random House, Copyright © 1994 by Sandra Cisneros: p. 100.

Printed in the United States of America

CONTENTS

Sandra Cisneros has traveled far from her origins as a poor Mexican-American girl living in a tough neighborhood, but she returns to it constantly, in both her award-winning books and her political activism.

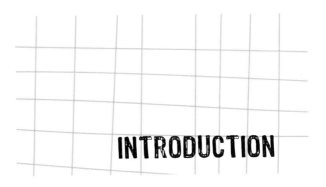

INTRODUCTION

SANDRA CISNEROS, THE ONLY DAUGHTER in a family of seven children, remembers her childhood as a lonely and painful time, not only because her family was constantly uprooted as it traveled between Mexico and the United States but also because of sexism, poverty, and racism. However, as a graduate student at the University of Iowa Writers' Workshop in the late 1970s, Cisneros discovered that being poor, female, and Mexican American was an advantage to her because these traits gave her an original writing voice. She used her experiences of growing up in a run-down, Mexican-American neighborhood in Chicago to write her first novel, *The House on Mango Street*, which appeared in 1984. She has also published three books of poetry, *Bad Boys*, *My Wicked Wicked Ways*, and *Loose Woman*; a collection of short stories, *Woman Hollering Creek and Other Stories*; a children's book, *Hairs/Pelitos*; and a second novel, *Caramelo*. Today Cisneros is one of the most popular and admired multicultural writers of the times. Besides being an active writer, Cisneros is also a dedicated activist who works tirelessly for Mexican-American causes. Like

Esperanza from *The House on Mango Street,* Cisneros has physically left her Chicago neighborhood, but she continually returns to Mexican-American communities in various cities to help minority women and men achieve the American dream. Her life mission can be summarized in Esperanza's final words: "I have gone away to come back. For the ones I left behind. For the ones who cannot get out."

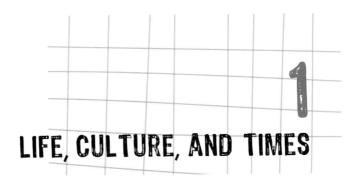

LIFE, CULTURE, AND TIMES

SANDRA CISNEROS'S MOST POPULAR BOOK, *The House on Mango Street*, is filled with stories from her childhood in Chicago, where she was born on December 20, 1954, into a rapidly changing society. She was less than a year old when a Baptist minister named Rev. Dr. Martin Luther King Jr. began protesting against discrimination, and Rosa Parks, an African-American seamstress in Montgomery, Alabama, refused to give up her bus seat to a white man. Of course, as a baby, Cisneros was unaware of King's demonstrations and Parks's defiant act. It is also doubtful whether she, as a very young girl in the early 1960s, knew that Chicana Joan Baez had won worldwide recognition as a folk singer or whether she paid attention to Gloria Steinem or Betty Friedan, who were working to advance women's equality. Yet the actions of these cultural leaders would help to foster the social changes that enabled Cisneros's career as a professional writer because mainstream Americans learned to value diversity and multiculturalism, opening publishing opportunities for minority female writers such as Cisneros.

Both the activism and the fame of Joan Baez would help Sandra Cisneros realize that she, too, could follow her dream of becoming a published writer.

Although, as a young elementary school student, Sandra Cisneros probably had no knowledge that early women's and civil rights leaders were paving the way for her to become a national figure who would be read and loved by Americans of all racial backgrounds, she was always aware that she was not a mainstream American but a Mexican American, a minority. She was raised with the cultures of two countries—Mexico and the United States—and she spoke two languages at home: English to her Mexican-American mother, who had been born in the United States to Mexican immigrants, and Spanish to her Mexican father. At home the Cisneros family did not call themselves Americans. The men usually referred to themselves as *Latinos*, while the women were *Latinas*, words defining people from the Spanish-speaking countries in North, Central, and South America. Sometimes they used the terms that refer exclusively to Mexican Americans: *Chicanos* for males and *Chicanas* for females. They never seemed to have called themselves *Hispanics*, a term, Cisneros feels, "erases the indigenous and African origins of the majority of people of Latin American origin."

Family

Cisneros's father, Alfredo Cisneros Del Moral, was born near Mexico City to a fairly wealthy and privileged family. Since Alfredo's father was a career military man, the Cisneros family received job-related benefits, including a college education for the children. Therefore, Alfredo enrolled in college, but, according to Cisneros, he "spent that first year gambling, and going after ladies, and having a good time" instead of studying. When he failed his classes, Cisneros says that rather than face his strict father, "he ran away like a prodigal son. Out of terror." He traveled around the United States until government officials "picked him up as an illegal alien [and] gave him the choice of being deported to Mexico or joining the United States Army" to fight in World War II. He chose to become a private in the army even though he could not speak English; in fact, Cisneros relates that he had "to ask the Puerto Ricans or any Spanish speakers in the Army what was going on."

When the war ended in 1945, Alfredo, now a U.S. citizen and an army veteran, continued drifting around the United States, accompanied by his brother, who had moved to the States a few years earlier. On one trip from New York to California, when the bus stopped in Chicago, Cisneros says that her father told his brother, "Well, I've heard there's lots of Mexicans here. Let's get off here for a little while." Their "little" visit stretched into lifetimes for both brothers, who ended up making their homes there.

Alfredo Cisneros stayed because he had fallen in love with Elvira, called Vera, Cordero Anguiano, a Mexican-American girl whom he had met at a dance. Elvira's parents, whom Cisneros describes as more "simple and much more humble" than Alfredo's, had come to the United States from Silao, Guanajuato, Mexico, during the Mexican Revolution of 1910 to escape from the violence. Cisneros's maternal grandmother described the situation as being so bad for the common people that those fighting both for and against the government would "steal your chickens and rape your women."

Sandra Cisneros's father, Alfredo, was born near Mexico City but served in the U.S. Army in World War II. He planned to return home, but fate intervened when he fell in love with Elvira during a visit to Chicago. The rest is history . . . and literature.

Searching for a better life, Cisneros's maternal grandfather found a job working for the railroad, "settling in Flagstaff, Kansas City, and finally Chicago where Vera was born." With her seven siblings, Vera was raised in a Mexican neighborhood, called a barrio, in Chicago, where the family spoke English, adopted American ways of life, and lost contact with relatives in Mexico. Although she was highly intelligent, Vera dropped out of school and labored as a factory worker.

After Alfredo and Vera married, Cisneros's father became a furniture upholsterer. In time, the couple had eight children, six sons and two daughters, but one daughter, Carolina, died in infancy, leaving Sandra as the only girl. She was the third child, having two older brothers, Alfred Junior and Henry, and four younger ones: Carlos, Arturo, Mario, and Armando.

As a child, Cisneros was often lonely. One reason was that she was unable to make long-term friends because her family moved to a new neighborhood yearly since her parents were poor. During the school months, the Cisneros family lived in Chicago, but every summer they "returned like the tides" to Mexico to stay with Alberto's parents in their roomy house in Oaxaca, the place Cisneros regards as "the only constant in the series of traumatic upheavals we experienced as children." Vacationing in Mexico and living in Chicago caused Cisneros to feel "almost like a foreigner" because "in some sense we're not Mexican and in some sense we're not American." Biographer Caryn Mirriam-Goldberg explains that "in Mexico, where she looked and sounded like a native, she was a visitor. In Chicago, outside her own neighborhood, she was a minority with an extra language and skin too dark to be seen as beautiful in American magazines or movies."

Because the family could not afford to pay rent during the months they were gone, they stored their belongings with Mrs. Cisneros's relatives. When they returned to Chicago in the late summer or early fall, they found a new apartment in a run-down barrio made up of Mexicans, Mexican Americans, and Puerto Ricans in the west or northwest side of Chicago. The nine members of the family crowded themselves into "small," "run-down" apartments "infested with cockroaches and mice," causing Cisneros, even as an adult, to describe herself as "terrified" of "[m]ice and any rodentia" because, she explains, "to me mice are all my poverty, the whole neighborhood I grew up in, embodied in a little skittering creature that might come to get me at any moment." The apartments were so small that Cisneros says she and her siblings slept "on the living room couch and fold-out Lazy Boy, and on beds set up in the middle room, where the only place with any privacy was the bathroom."

In spite of living in crowded conditions as part of a large family that loved her, Cisneros was lonely at home. Her brothers didn't let her play with them, instead pairing up in three groups of two. Cisneros says that her brothers "excluded me from their games" and "had their own conspiracies and allegiances, leaving me odd-woman-out forever." Furthermore, her loving father would sometimes act as if his daughter did not count, telling people, "I have seven sons," and not bothering to correct his statement even when his little daughter would tug his sleeve and whisper, "Not seven sons. Six! and *one daughter*." In spite of her father's statement, Cisneros was

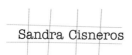
always aware that she was her father's precious little girl, "his favorite," as she said, even though he held the sexist idea that girls were not as important as boys.

Besides excluding her, Cisneros's father and brothers isolated her from others by being overly protective of her. Cisneros's Mexican father believed that it was the duty of men to protect women. With what Cisneros calls "seven fathers" guarding her, she felt caged but secure, a "pampered only daughter with six brothers." In later years she recognized "that part of the reason my father trapped me and kept my brothers protecting me, all of them telling me I was a princess, was that he loved me so much. He wanted me to be in a little bubble."

Because she lived in a male-dominated household and in a patriarchal society, Cisneros could have become a traditional passive Mexican-American woman: guided by her father until she married and ruled by her husband after the wedding. In an interview with Pilar E. Rodriguez Aranda, Cisneros describes this cultural expectation in this way: "I guess as Mexican daughters we're not supposed to have our own house. We have our father's house and then he hands us over to our husband's." Any female growing up in the 1960s faced great difficulties if she wanted to live an independent life, a situation made more difficult for Cisneros because she was not only female but also poor and Mexican American. The decade of the 1960s was a time before women's rights were recognized—it was a time of male domination, especially in Latino cultures, and of white domination. Cisneros was very fortunate to have a mother who encouraged her to follow an independent way of life.

Although Vera Cisneros had quit school before she finished ninth grade, she was "a freethinker, very bright, an amazing and extraordinary Latina woman" who loved books, sang "Puccini opera," and knew how to cook "a dinner for nine with only five dollars." Cisneros says her mother sacrificed her own dreams of a creative life to take care of her husband and children. She describes her mother as "a prisoner of war. She was captured, she didn't want to be there, she was unhappy, she was banging away in the kitchen, the way that a prisoner would bang on her jail cell, you know, really unhappy. She had to cook for nine people with really little money, so she really just got burned out." Explaining that her mother "didn't want me to inherit her sadness and her rolling pin," Cisneros says Vera Cisneros "herded her kids weekly to the library, to public concerts, to museums" to make sure that her children were exposed to cultural materials. Cisneros believes that "if it weren't for her, my brothers [who became a doctor, an artist, a musician, a geologist, and business owners] and I would not be the creative individuals we are."

Not only did Vera Cisneros introduce her daughter to the arts, she also made sure she had time to be creative and to study, never burdening her with child care or housework. Cisneros relates, "Because of my mother, I spent my childhood afternoons in my own room reading instead of in the kitchen. . . . I never had to change my little brothers' diapers, I never had to cook a meal alone, nor was I ever sent to do the laundry." Therefore, as a child Cisneros "was always creating, imagining and inventing. I was an artist. I spent a lot of time daydreaming." By the time she was in elementary

Sandra Cisneros credits her mother with putting her dreams aside so that her children could realize theirs.

school, Cisneros was writing stories. As she relates in later life, "I'd been writing stories since grammar school." Vera Cisneros "always supported the daughter's projects, as long as she went to school," in later years often telling her successful, independent daughter, "Good lucky you studied."

Although the impoverished family owned only two books—a Bible and an old copy of *Alice in Wonderland*—Vera Cisneros made sure her daughter read library books, which the young girl thought "were so valuable as to only be dispensed to institutions and libraries, the only place I'd seen them." One of Cisneros's favorite fairy tales was Hans Christian Andersen's "Six Swans," the story of a girl who rescues her many brothers from a magic charm that changed them into swans. Years later, Cisneros explained that she was obsessed with this book because she closely identified with Andersen's girl since her "family name [Cisneros] translated as "keeper of swans'" and because she saw herself as a type of ugly duckling that was "ridiculous, ugly, perennially the new kid. But one day the spell would wear off."

An even more beloved work was Virginia Lee Burton's *The Little House*, a picture book about a dearly loved house that was part of a family for generations. A permanent home appealed to Cisneros, who found *"The Little House* the house I dreamed of, a house where one family lived and didn't move." This book was so important to her that she and one of her brothers schemed to tell the library they had lost the book so they could keep it. "That was the plan," Cisneros claims, "a good one, but never executed—good, guilty Catholics that we were."

Cisneros's dream of a permanent home became reality in

1966 when she was eleven years old. Her parents bought their first house in the Humboldt Park area of Chicago—1525 North Campbell Street. The young girl had yearned for a real house for years, imagining it to be a luxurious, spacious place. But this "small, ugly two-story bungalow in one of Chicago's Puerto Rican neighborhoods" was nothing like her dream. Although she was greatly disappointed in the house, she did at last have a room of her own that she describes as "a narrow closet just big enough for my twin bed and an oversized blond dresser we'd bought in the bargain basement of *el Sears*," a piece of furniture as "long as a coffin" that did not allow her to shut her bedroom door. Even so, with a room of her own, Cisneros now had a quiet place to read and write.

Education

Because of the family's frequent trips to Mexico, Cisneros attended a new school almost yearly as an elementary school student. After going to public school for the first year and a half, she was enrolled in various Catholic schools, not because the family was religious but because her parents believed that the private schools offered a better education. Cisneros, however, did not like her elementary schools. She detested the buildings that to her looked like prisons, "big, hulky, and authoritarian, the kind of architecture meant to instill terror." Also, she was often terrified by the nuns, who, she says, "were majestic at making one feel little" as they tried to instill in her the idea that "[g]irls, and especially poor Mexican-American girls, were not supposed to read, write, and study so much." To make matters worse,

St. Callistus, one of Cisneros's earliest schools, was, according to Cisneros, "very racist," split between "the Italian kids [who] dominated the schools and Latinos like herself [who] were the minority." School became better for Cisneros after the family purchased its first house and she transferred to St. Aloysius Elementary School. Here the nuns encouraged her to read because, Cisneros says, "[t]hey recognized that I was doing all this reading outside of class and that I was smart."

Cisneros started becoming a serious writer at Josephinum High School, a Catholic all-girls school, which she entered in 1968. She had a lot of time to devote to writing because she had no boyfriend since no boy was interested in her. She later observed that not having a boyfriend was a good thing because her life could have been very different. She writes, "I would have thrown myself into love the way some warriors throw themselves into fighting. I was ready to sacrifice everything in the name of love, to do anything, even risk my own life." In her sophomore year, Cisneros, inspired by a teacher who wrote poetry and encouraged her students to do creative writing, wrote poems she described as "filled with pleas for peace and saving the environment" and "a few catchy words like ecology and Coca-Cola." By Cisneros's senior year, the other students considered Cisneros the class poet and applauded her work as an editor of the school's creative-writing magazine.

Before she graduated from high school in 1972, Cisneros had decided to attend college, a bold choice for a poor Chicana who was expected to marry young because, according to her cultural expectations, "daughters were meant for

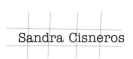

husbands." Ever since she was a young child, Cisneros had dreamed of going to college, telling her father of her plans when she was only a fifth grader: "I remember my father saying, '*Que bueno, mi'ja,* that's good.' That meant a lot to me, especially since my brothers thought the idea hilarious." As Cisneros was finishing high school, her brothers once again laughed at her for desiring to go to college, but her father was pleased with her decision, thinking, as Cisneros discovered later, that college would be an ideal place for her to find a good husband. Reflecting on her situation, Cisneros wrote, "I'm lucky my father believed daughters were meant for husbands. It meant it didn't matter if I majored in something silly like English."

In the fall of 1972, Cisneros received a scholarship to Loyola University in Chicago and enrolled in this Jesuit Catholic college. Although she was one of the few minority students, she was accepted by her classmates and enjoyed college much more than high school. She loved studying literature, but the class that made the greatest impact on her was a creative-writing workshop in which she enrolled during her junior year. Every week she was required to write fiction or poetry and share her work with her fellow students.

Recognizing that her writing greatly improved when she heard comments from other writers, Cisneros looked for a graduate school in which she would have similar opportunities. The University of Iowa, a university that was and still is highly prestigious and hard to get into, seemed to be the ideal place. Not only did it have the Iowa Writers' Workshop, but it also employed two of her favorite poets as professors: Donald Justice and Marvin Bell. Therefore, after she graduated from Loyola in the spring of 1976, Cisneros moved away from home for the first time in her life. She went to Ames, Iowa, and began working on a master of fine arts degree in creative writing.

Cisneros hated the two years she spent at the Iowa Writers' Workshop, telling an interviewer that it "was deadly for me." For one thing, she was disappointed when she discovered that both poet-professors had taken the year off to work on their own writings. In addition, she felt lonely and isolated from her fellow classmates, who were, for the most part, wealthy and white. Worse yet, the Iowa Writers' Workshop did not appeal to her; she found the program "terribly cruel to her as well as to many of the other first-year students." Biographer Caryn Mirriam-Goldberg explains that Cisneros felt this way because "[t]here was competition, tremendous pressure to produce great writing, and additional pressure to make lasting connections with prominent writers." Because of the intense competition, her classmates were not interested in helping one another succeed, and Cisneros quickly realized "that nobody cared to hear what I had to say and no one listened to me even when I did speak," causing her to become "very frightened and terrified that first year."

In spite of her frustrations with the university, the students, and the Iowa Writers' Workshop, Cisneros greatly benefited from her education there. At the workshop, she learned that her writing voice was unique, a realization she stumbled upon during a time of great frustration. It began one day when Cisneros's class was analyzing the way

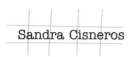
one author used houses to represent the inner lives of people. Although Cisneros's classmates liked the symbolism, feeling that houses represented their self-identity and imagination, Cisneros could not relate, finding the idea repugnant that her soul was represented by her parents' ugly, crowded house, which she regarded as "a prison for me." Realizing that she was different and did not fit into the norm was a defining moment in her life: "It was not until this moment when I separated myself, when I considered myself truly distinct, that my writing acquired a voice. . . . I knew I was a Mexican woman. But, I didn't think it had anything to do with why I felt so much imbalances in my life, whereas it had everything to do with it! . . . It had been as if all of the sudden I realized, 'Oh, my god! Here's something [poverty] that my classmates can't write about, and I'm going to tell you because I'm the authority on this—I can tell you.'"

With this breakthrough, Cisneros began writing about "third-floor flats, and fear of rats, and drunk husbands sending rocks through windows," and she adopted the distinctive Latina, poor, female voice that none of her classmates could copy. With her decision to write about things she had encountered, "*The House on Mango Street* was born, the child-voice that was to speak all my poems for many years." She also wrote poetry using her new subject matter and voice, collecting them into a volume for her master's thesis, which she called "My Wicked Wicked Ways."

Cisneros received other benefits by attending the University of Iowa. Several of her teachers supported and encouraged her. She made two good friends: Joy Harjo, a Creek Indian who grew up on an American Indian reserva-

At the University of Iowa, Cisneros discovered the works of other female minority writers, among them the trailblazing African-American writer Toni Morrison.

tion in Oklahoma, and Dennis Mathis, a fiction writer who "would become [a] life-long editor, ally, and voice on the phone when either one of us lost heart." And she discovered literature written by minority authors, finding particular delight in the writings of Chinese-American writer Maxine Hong Kingston, African-American novelist Toni Morrison, and Chicano poet Gary Soto.

Work

After she graduated from the University of Iowa with an MFA in Creative Writing in May 1978, Cisneros, at age twenty-three and a half, returned to her father's house in Chicago. "Now she summoned her courage and told her father she wanted to live alone again" even though she knew that in her culture "sons and daughters don't leave their parents' house until they marry." Her father, having worked hard all his life, wanted his daughter to become eco-

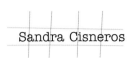
nomically stable and follow roles he regarded as traditional: "to be a weather girl on television, or to marry and have babies." But Cisneros realized that "there are so many other things she must do in her lifetime first. Travel. Learn how to dance the tango. Publish a book. Live in other cities. Win a National Endowment for the Arts award. See the Northern Lights. Jump out of a cake."

Not wanting "to live a life filled with regrets" as her mother had done, Cisneros soon was living in an apartment of her own and teaching at Latino Youth Alternative High School in Chicago's poverty-stricken South Side. This was a school for students who did not fit into a traditional high school. Many had dropped out of school; some had learning disabilities; some were homeless after leaving traumatic family situations; many girls were pregnant or had young children; a number of students were abusing drugs or alcohol; and many were in trouble with the law. Cisneros helped these troubled teenagers earn their high school diplomas and search for jobs. With such demanding work, she had little creative energy, but she did manage to give poetry readings at bars and coffeehouses. As her local fame grew, the Chicago Transit Authority featured one of her poems on buses and train cars, sharing her words with thousands of commuters.

With this newfound attention, Cisneros was able to meet Gary Soto, who, in 1980, helped her publish her first book, *Bad Boys*, in the Chicano Chapbook series he edited for Mango Press. (A chapbook is a short collection of poetry.) Consisting of seven poems about her life in the barrio that had been part of her master's thesis, Cisneros described her chapbook as a work that was "four pages long and was bound together on a kitchen table with a stapler and a spoon."

Having one book in print whetted Cisneros's desire to get more works published. In particular, she wanted to shape stories based on her home on Campbell Street, where she had lived during her middle and high school years, into a novel that she planned to call *The House on Mango Street*. She believed that each work could "stand alone while also being part of a larger story" because "[y]ou would understand each story like a little pearl, or you could look at the whole thing like a necklace. . . . That's what I always knew from the day that I wrote the first one. I said, 'I'm going to do a whole series of these, and it's going to be like this, and it'll all be connected.'"

In order to have time to work on this novel, Cisneros took a less demanding job at Loyola University early in 1980, working as a counselor-recruiter for the Educational Opportunity Program, which helped disadvantaged students. During this time, she met her first serious boyfriend, a Caucasian who wanted to marry her and settle down in the suburbs. This life did not appeal to Cisneros at all because she did not want to marry. One reason she felt that way was that she had never witnessed a happy marriage. In a 1990 interview with Aranda, Cisneros explained, "I've never seen a model of a happy marriage. Or I've never seen a marriage that is as happy as my living alone, I've never seen it!" Cisneros's second reason for not wanting to marry was that she feared that all of her creative time would be lost in caring for a family. Understandably, her relationship with this boyfriend did not last.

In 1982, Nicolás Kanellos, the publisher of Arte Público Press, a small, "federally funded press whose mandate had been to place in bookshelves the fiction by Latinos that mainstream New York publishers refused to endorse," showed an interest in publishing Cisneros's novel. The use of federal money to publish the works of Mexican-American writers came about as a result of the multicultural movement that was sweeping the country. Cultural critic Ilan Stavans, a Mexican Jew who is a professor of Spanish at Amherst College, declares that "[b]y the late eighties, multiculturalism had become a national obsession."

Great interest in diversity and, as a result, in the writings of minorities began after African Americans brought the issue of inequality to the nation's attention with the civil rights movement that began in 1955 when Cisneros was a baby. By the early 1960s, historian Oscar Handlin wrote that Rev. Dr. Martin Luther King Jr. had made the black civil rights movement "the main domestic issue in the United States." This "drive for equality that began with blacks spread to other minority groups," including Latinos. They had migrated to America en masse in the late 1950s and 1960s as a result of two events that occurred in 1959 when Cisneros was a little girl: the Cuban Revolution, which resulted in Fidel Castro taking control of the government, and the establishment of the Trujillo dictatorship in the Dominican Republic. As a result, Latinos "became a visible part of American social and political life in the 1960s," and the Chicano Movement was started. It helped instill "racial and cultural pride" for Mexican Americans who advocated not only for economic reforms but also for cultural opportunities. Because of these civil rights movements, minority writers such as Cisneros began to have many more opportunities to get their books published.

Cisneros was also helped in her publication efforts by the women's rights movement. Two women were especially influential in bringing the inequalities of women to light. One was Gloria Steinem. In an article published in *Esquire* magazine in 1962, when Cisneros was in elementary school, Steinem criticized the limitations placed on women because they had to choose between a career and marriage. She later

Cisneros came of age with the women's movement. The efforts of feminists such as Gloria Steinem—here seen at her desk at *Ms.* magazine, which she founded—made it easier for women's voices to be heard.

founded the feminist magazine *Ms.* The other activist was Betty Friedan. In *The Feminine Mystique*, published in 1963, Friedan attacked society for treating women as second-class citizens. Under the leadership of these two women, feminists worked for strict enforcement of laws and advocated measures to promote equality for women. According to critics Bridget Kevane and Juanita Heredia, as a result of "the Chicano, civil rights, Puerto Rican, and women's movements, Latinas made inroads into American society. Because of the social activism and institutional reforms that were an outgrowth of these movements, Latinas gained access to an educational system that enabled them to develop careers as writers and academics. . . . If it were not for the social movements of the 1960s, it is doubtful whether U.S. Latina literature would exist today."

In 1982, Cisneros was able to take advantage of the demand for Latina literature. After she received a huge grant from the National Endowment for the Arts, she had enough money to live on for at least a year and began to work earnestly to complete her novel so it could be published by Kanellos. That summer she left her job at Loyola to spend her time writing and traveling. She first went to Provincetown, Massachusetts, to get help with her novel from Dennis Mathis, whom she calls "the most wonderful friend and my literary mentor." Although she worked throughout the summer, she did not finish the book by Kanellos's deadline and asked for more time.

To get a change of scenery, she traveled to Greece that fall, where she finished the first draft of her novel at "4 AM on the day of her second deadline, November 30, 1982."

When Kanellos received the manuscript, he asked Cisneros to revise the book, feeling that it was not "quite there." For the next year and a half, Cisneros kept rewriting her novel, as well as revising the poems she had written for her master's thesis and composing new poems for a book collection she would call *My Wicked Wicked Ways*. During this time, she frequently moved around Europe, visiting Paris and living in the south of France before going to Italy and settling in Venice in the spring of 1983. To help meet her expenses, she became an artist-in-residence at the Michael Karolyi Artist's Foundation in Venice, receiving living expenses in exchange for teaching a few hours a week.

She spent the summer of 1983 in Sarajevo, Yugoslavia (now Bosnia), where she lived with her boyfriend, performing a role she later described as "being a wife": "I washed shirts by hand; with a broom and bucket of suds I scrubbed the tiles of the garden each morning from all the pigeon droppings that fell from the flock that lived on the roof of the garden shed." Her experiences of the summer helped strengthen her resolve never to marry. Instead of serving a husband and family, she determined to dedicate her time and energy to writing. In Sarajevo, Cisneros met a woman named Jasna Karaula, who would become a lifelong friend and a translator of some of her works.

When Cisneros finally completed her revisions of *The House on Mango Street* in 1984 after more than six years of work, she returned to the United States in order to be on hand when the novel was published. The reviews pleased the twenty-nine-year-old author; critics saw her work as "poetic and very touching," and they praised its moving dialogue and strong descriptions. Cisneros was awarded an Illinois Artists Grant in 1984, and in 1985, the novel was awarded the Before Columbus Foundation's American Book Award. It was also adopted as required reading in many colleges and universities because, according to editor Nicolás Kanellos, Cisneros was "part of the early wave of Hispanic writers who helped supply the books for the often controversial ethnic and women's studies programs added to the university curriculums in the 1970s and 1980s."

In spite of the novel's success, Cisneros did not earn enough money to support herself with her writing, so she looked for employment. In the fall of 1984, she found a job in San Antonio, Texas, as the arts administrator at the Guadalupe Cultural Arts Center. Cisneros immediately felt at home living in this city with its large community of Spanish-speaking Mexican Americans, Mexicans, and Latin Americans. Biographer Virginia Brackett claims that Cisneros, "[f]or the first time, felt that she actually fit into a community. She felt comfortable living as a Chicana so close to the country of Mexico. In addition, San Antonio as a whole did value the arts, even the arts of Mexican Americans. . . . Spanish words floated around constantly, and she gained a new appreciation for the rhythms of the language." She eagerly became involved in the Chicana community, working to highlight the arts produced by her people.

Although she liked her job and her volunteer work, Cisneros was, once again, frustrated because she did not have time to write. But soon after her arrival, she was awarded the Texas Institute of Letters Dobie-Paisano Fellowship, which gave her a monetary stipend and provided her with a quiet place to live on a ranch near Austin. For six months, Cisneros was able to write without worrying about making money. Living here, she felt an even closer attachment to Texas: "a landscape that matches the one inside me, one foot in this country, one in that. Graceful two-step, howl of an accordion, little gem and jewel, a little sad, a little joyous, that has made me whole. A place where two languages coexist, two cultures side by side . . . [in] that homeland called the heart."

When the fellowship expired, Cisneros returned to San Antonio. Even though she received the Chicano Short Story Award from the University of Arizona in 1986 and *The House on Mango Street* went into its third printing in 1987, Cisneros did not earn enough money to pay her bills. Not wanting to leave San Antonio, she let "her waiter boyfriend support her for months" as she desperately sought work as a creative-writing teacher. But she soon realized she would have to find a steady job elsewhere. When California State University in Chico offered her a one-year position as a visiting lecturer to teach creative-writing classes, she took the job, moving to California in the fall of 1987.

Although Cisneros was relieved to have an income, biographer Caryn Mirriam-Goldberg writes that "[l]eaving San Antonio was heart-wrenching for Cisneros, and she became increasingly depressed." Part of her depression was caused by her job, work she had assumed would be quite easy and leave her plenty of time to write. But she quickly found that teaching at the university was like "marriage. It's like giving up freedom." Preparing for classes, teaching, and grading were "exhausting, as exhausting as factory work, except I work more hours and get paid more." She lamented that "my private time gets stolen because I can't write. My creativity is going towards . . . [my students] and to my teaching and to my one-on-one with them. I never find a balance."

Besides finding the work grueling and time-consuming, Cisneros, according to biographers Virginia Brackett and Caryn Mirriam-Goldberg, was also frustrated with university timelines and students' criticisms of her. She did not like to be confined by class starting and stopping times. Because she "habitually arrived late" to her classes, students who attended class on time complained because, as Brackett explains, they "felt that she did not respect them when she came in late." When the bell rang at the end of the class period, Cisneros did not want to dismiss students; she wanted them to stay to continue their unfinished writing and to listen to her as she shared her ideas. It was disturbing to her "that students had to stop writing, sometimes in mid-sentence" as they packed up their work and left for their next classes.

Discouraged with her job, unhappy with not having time to write, disappointed that her novel had not been more successful financially, and homesick for San Antonio, Cisneros was miserable, trapped in a life she hated. She soon fell into acute depression and lost all confidence in herself, both as a teacher and as a writer, even refusing to call a literary agent who was interested in helping her publish another work of fiction. Cisneros later told an interviewer, "I thought I couldn't teach. I found myself becoming suicidal. . . . It was frightening because it was such a calm depression."

Adding to her depression was the poor reception of her third book, *My Wicked Wicked Ways*. This is an expansion of her master's thesis that consists of a collection of sixty poems dealing with love, sex, and identity that she had begun writing as a graduate student in 1978. Cisneros selected the title because she considered herself a "sort of resistance fighter," a wicked "daughter to fight for the right of a life of letters—it was a wicked act, to defy everything that was destined for me, what my father thought was best. To live by myself was wicked, and I had to fight my father and older brother just to live alone."

When Third Woman Press, an independent company that printed works written by minority women, released the book in 1987, readers did not find the subject matter wicked or controversial, but the cover photo of Cisneros created a sensation. She was dressed to look like a sexual temptress—holding a cigarette in her hand, sitting cross-legged with a glass of red wine near her, and wearing a slinky dress, cowboy boots, and red earrings that matched her bright red lips. Biographer Virginia Brackett writes, "Men complained that she led them on, as she appeared to be promising a sexual experience of sorts. Some feminists expressed disapproval that Cisneros offered herself in the stereotyped image of a woman whose only importance was as a sex object." Cisneros defended the photo, asking, "And why can't a feminist be sexy? Sexiness, I think, [is] a great feeling of self-empowerment." Upset that the book was not well received and realizing that "no one seemed to care about poetry anyway [because] it wasn't as if people were banging down the door for my poems," Cisneros decided she would never publish any more poetry; however, she changed her mind a few years later.

In 1988, despite the poor reception of her newest book, Cisneros finally contacted Susan Bergholz, "a Manhattan literary agent making a niche for emerging Latino literati" who, according to cultural critic Ilan Stavans, were in demand because of the increased interest in Latino literature by college and university professors who advocated for "diversity and the politics of inclusion." Critic Ellen McCracken explains that this demand came about because of major social pressures in the 1980s that "catalyzed the boom in publication of fiction by Latina women. As militant movements continued to demand an end to the myth of the melting pot, corporations and institutions sought ways to pacify, limit, and even profit from the social unrest. Universities established departments of ethnic studies, and one by one mainstream publishing houses . . . offered book contracts to selected Latina writers in the late 1980s and 1990s, aware that there was now a large audience of minority and non-minority readers interested in ethnic fiction."

When Bergholz asked Cisneros to give her copies of new fiction, Cisneros sent thirty-nine pages of stories. Based on this small sample, Bergholz sold Cisneros's uncompleted story collection, which would be titled *Woman Hollering Creek and Other Stories*, to a major publishing company, Random House, for a $100,000 advance payment, the largest ever received by a Chicano writer. According to McCracken, this was a "key accomplishment." Bergholz also arranged for Vintage Books, a division of Random House, to reissue *The House on Mango Street*. Thus, with the help of her agent, Cisneros soon became a major representative of the Latino minority at a time when "a spokesfigure for the brewing Latino minority was urgently needed. . . . With the help of the right promotional machinery, she moved to center stage."

Cisneros's confidence got another big boost when she was awarded a second National Endowment for the Arts Fellowship in fiction in 1988. With the financial independence that came with the grant, Cisneros was able to leave her teaching job and concentrate solely on her writing.

For the next three years, Cisneros slaved over *Woman Hollering Creek*, trying to complete her stories to meet her publisher's deadline, sometimes working twelve hours a day. When the money from her advance and from the National Endowment for the Arts Fellowship ran out, Cisneros took temporary jobs, serving for a week or longer as a guest professor—giving readings of her works, working with students in creative-writing workshops, and discussing the life of a writer with students and faculty—at various colleges and universities, including the University of California, Berkeley, in 1988; the University of California, Irvine, in 1990; the University of Michigan, Ann Arbor (where she finished *Woman Hollering Creek*), in 1990; and the University of New Mexico, Albuquerque, in 1991.

Writing and Serving

In 1991, when Cisneros was thirty-six years old, *Woman Hollering Creek and Other Stories*, a collection of twenty-two short stories about Mexican-American women living in and around San Antonio, was published by Random House, an event that, according to biographer Virginia Brackett, marked "a milestone in Cisneros's career, and also in the world of publishing. With it, Cisneros had crossed over into the mainstream press, and because of this, many more readers would have the chance to encounter her work. A few Chicano writers . . . had crossed over into the mainstream previously, but no Chicana had ever done so." Eagerly bought by readers and praised by critics, *Woman Hollering Creek* received the PEN Center West Award for Best Fiction of 1991 and the prestigious and lucrative Lannan Foundation Literary Award for Fiction, a prize of $50,000 given annually for exceptional works of fiction.

With the success of *Woman Hollering Creek* and with the 1991 reissuing of *The House on Mango Street* by Vintage Books, Cisneros no longer had doubts about her talent. It had been thirteen years since she had graduated from the University of Iowa, years spent struggling to support herself by working in one temporary job after another. Those days were now behind her.

She immediately bought a small, hundred-year-old Victorian house in the prosperous King William Historic District of San Antonio. Cisneros relished the privacy and independence she had in her own house: "Sometimes all I want to do is turn the music on, walk around the house, dance by myself, do somersaults, and I don't want someone looking at me doing that. . . . Or I need to cry or I want to laugh aloud and I don't want to explain why I'm laughing or why I'm crying."

In 1991, she also purchased a bright red pickup truck, a vehicle she calls "a *real* car" in *Woman Hollering Creek*. She decorated it colorfully, placing Mexican fabric on the seats and fringe around the windshield. When her father saw that his daughter had money to buy a truck, he finally began to take her career seriously. At Christmastime in 1991, Cisneros, who was visiting with her father in Chicago when he was bedridden because of the stroke he had suffered in 1989, shared one of her stories that had recently been translated into Spanish. Her father stopped watching his soap operas on television to read her whole story, laughing at some of the incidents and reading sections aloud. When he was through, he asked her, "Where can we get more copies of this for the relatives?"

Cisneros changed her mind about not publishing any more poetry, and in 1992, Random House reissued *My Wicked Wicked Ways*, placing her poetry in mainstream America and assuring her success as a writer. The publisher also gave her advance payments for two new works: a collection of poetry, *Loose Woman*, and a novel based on the lives of her father's relatives, *Caramelo*.

Having achieved national fame, Cisneros wanted to further her involvement in her community, not only through her stories but also by actively promoting other Latino artists. In late 1992, she traveled to the International Festival of Books in Guadalajara, Mexico, to challenge publishers to print more works by Mexican-American women, noting that "she was the only Chicana in the world able to support herself with her writing." That same year she refused to pose for an advertisement for a major clothing store, Gap, because the company was not helping Latinos as much as it could. The following year she took a similar stand for her people "when a bookstore owner in north Texas invited

Cisneros to come to his store for a reading, [and] she discovered he had never invited any other Latino writers in the past. She refused to go unless he asked other Latino writers to join her."

As part of her ongoing commitment to address matters of social justice and to advance social change, Cisneros helped her friend Jasna Karaula, who wrote to her in 1993 telling of Sarajevo's devastation during the Bosnian war: the people had no running water, lacked food and fuel, and were dying of cold and living in fear. Cisneros circulated her friend's letter to major newspapers and pleaded for the United States to intervene in Bosnia. From 1993 until 1996, she held weekly peace vigils for her friend, who still lived in Sarajevo.

Meanwhile, Cisneros continued to receive accolades for her writings. In 1993, she was awarded the Ansfield-Wolf Book Award for *Woman Hollering Creek*, an award given to a few writers whose works help the general public appreciate and understand diversity of cultures. She was also given an honorary Doctor of Letters degree from the State University of New York at Purchase.

In 1994, Cisneros had two new books published by Knopf, a division of Random House: *Hairs/Pelitos*, a book for children ages four to eight that consists of one of the chapters from *The House on Mango Street*; and *Loose Woman*, a book of "flagrantly erotic" poetry. In spite of Cisneros's assessment that these poems were "too dangerous to publish in my lifetime" because she talked about things a person does not normally share with others, she was upset over the "vitriolic" reviews of her book and suffered a "very adverse reaction when *Loose Woman* came out in Texas. It received almost no reviews. The one or two reviews it received were so negative and so hurtful to me that I thought, why am I writing poetry for anyone?"

By this time Cisneros was working on her novel *Cara-melo*. Although she had started writing it in 1993, the work progressed slowly because Cisneros was busy with many other projects during the 1990s: reading selections from *Caramelo* to public audiences, twice going on book tours in Europe to promote the European publication of *Loose Woman*, giving lectures and speeches, and volunteering in her community. In 1995, she hosted a Macondo Writing Workshop, named after the town in which Gabriel Marquez's novel *One Hundred Years of Solitude* is set. The workshop was made up of a group of poets, novelists, journalists, performance artists, and creative writers who worked to bring about social change through nonviolent means, believing "that arts should serve our communities."

Cisneros became a national celebrity in 1995 when she was awarded a $225,000 MacArthur Foundation Fellowship. These fellowships, commonly referred to as "genius grants," are given annually to artistically and intellectually creative people who show exceptional accomplishment and promise. This grant was beneficial to her in several ways. Because of the MacArthur Foundation's financial assistance, she was given "wings that allowed the manuscript [of *Cara-melo*] to take flight and become the book I saw in my heart." Furthermore, because she was nationally famous after winning this prestigious fellowship, she was able to obtain more money for her work, receiving $10,000 for public readings, huge advance payments for books, and large stipends as an artist-in-resident conducting workshops at colleges and universities. With financial independence came "peace of mind," a "kind of security."

The MacArthur fellowship also helped her psychologically. Cisneros felt she no longer needed to prove her worth as a writer: "Those who still had doubts about whether I was a real writer or not must be quiet. . . . I don't need the university any more. Now I am a certified person. I am the real thing now as a writer. It also meant I don't need to work for awards anymore. The awards were important to me, for the credibility."

In addition, the MacArthur helped her emotionally. She told an interviewer, "The best gift the MacArthur gave me— my father," explaining that because she received the money, "he understands the level of my success, and he understands why I did it. It's so wonderful that he's lived long enough so that now he says *la novella*, the novel, instead of when are you going to get married? That's what he used to say. Now it's 'Don't get married because they only want your money.'"

With the MacArthur fellowship, Cisneros now had the money and time to devote herself to *Caramelo*, but she was derailed from completing the novel in the 1990s because of the illness and death of her beloved father, who, Cisneros says, was "very dear and close to me, a companion of the heart." In 1995, he had quadruple bypass surgery; the following year he was diagnosed with terminal cancer. Cisneros says she "had to take off nine months when my father was ill, . . . and the MacArthur gave me the luxury of stopping everything and being with my father during that time." It was a difficult time for the author who "watched him dissolve before my eyes. Each day the cancer that was eating him changed his face, as if he was crumbling from within and turning into a sugar skull, the kind placed on altars for Day of the Dead." When he died on February 12, 1997, Cisneros felt the loss intensely, describing her pain as "having a knife pulled out of your eye." She felt that "a piece of my heart died with him. My father, that supreme sentimental fool, loved my brothers and me to excess in a kind of over-the-top rococo fever, all arabesques and sugar spirals, as sappy and charming as the romantic Mexican boleros he loved to sing." For years after his death, Cisneros suffered writer's block.

Although she experienced "inevitable loss" when her father died, she also found "inevitable gain" as she, in the months after his death, became aware of another world she calls "the spirituality of my ancestors." She explains that "when you lose a loved one, you suddenly have a spirit ally, an energy on the other side that is with you always, that is with you just by calling their name. I know my father watches over me in a much more thorough way than he ever could when he was alive. . . . Now I simply summon him in my thoughts. Papa. Instantly, I feel his presence surround and calm me." She feels that her dead father "inspires me now to be creative in ways I never realized" and that his "kindness and generosity teach me to enlarge my heart."

With her awareness of a spiritual world, Cisneros sought religious guidance and soon became "a Buddhist who believes in compassion, nonviolence, and 'putting my writing to service.'" Desiring to publicly proclaim her spiritual beliefs, Cisneros, around the turn of the century, got a tattoo on her arm, a design she calls the Buddha Lupe— a combination of Buddha and the Virgin of Guadalupe, a "religious icon around which Mexican Catholicism centers" that is traditionally regarded as "the consolation of the poor, the shield of the weak, the help of the oppressed." Cisneros, however, views the Virgin of Guadalupe as "a very powerful, sexual goddess, a symbol of creative destructiveness." The fused figures that make up the Buddha Lupe represent to Cisneros "that guidance and love we get when we open up our hearts and are guided by our higher selves, or God, or the Buddha Lupe."

A few months after her father's death, Cisneros became embroiled in a prolonged fight with the city of San Antonio about the color of her house, which she painted periwinkle in May 1997, a color many saw as a "vivid, intense, in-your-face shade of purple." Historical commission officials, finding that she had violated the community's bylaws about paint colors acceptable in an historic district, wanted her to repaint her house. However, Cisneros maintained that the neon purple honored her Mexican ancestors who had lived in this area, and she argued that the commissioners were "narrow minded and ethnically exclusionary." In August, Cisneros brought the issue to national attention and soon a "retinue of ardent feminists, gays, artists, writers, and adoring fans" began showing their support by tying purple ribbons in trees. In spite of the bad publicity, the city of San Antonio refused to back down until Cisneros agreed to paint her house an accepted shade of pink. But, more than a year later, in October 1998, her house was still purple, although it had faded

Even in her house color, Cisneros has been a radical. Her infamous purple house roused the city of San Antonio against her. In the end, she felt that the brawl was a triumph, not just for her but for Mexican Americans everywhere.

to violet, a color the commission found acceptable. Even though this fight took a great deal of time, Cisneros felt that the struggle was worthwhile because it made people aware of Mexican Americans and their history.

Meanwhile, Cisneros continued to work for the Latino community. In November 1997, "in part to make [her father's] life count," she worked with community volunteers to organize a reunion of Latino/a MacArthur Fellows that she called Los MacArturos. The group met in San Antonio, hosting free workshops, lectures, and discussions to share the members' expertise with the Mexican-American community. The next month she participated in Chicago's Near West Side neighborhood's literary program, the Writ-

er's Voice. In appreciation of her work, the Mexican Fine Arts Center Museum in Chicago honored her with a lifetime achievement award in 1998. Besides promoting the arts and education, Cisneros also campaigned to end capital punishment in 2000. However, her biggest community commitment was to her fellow Chicano writers. In 2000, she established a grant-giving institution to serve Texas writers, which she named the Alfredo Cisneros Del Moral Foundation in honor of her father.

After a decade of work, Cisneros finally completed *Caramelo* in 2002, dedicating the book to her father: "Para ti, Papá." It was published by Knopf in October of that year. Cisneros was pleased with this book, telling an interviewer, "I tried my very best . . . So I'm happy." The critics eagerly embraced it, hailing it as "a joyful, fizzy novel, a deliciously subversive reminder that 'American' applies to plenty of territory beyond the borders of the United States." Critic Ellen McCracken praised the book for bringing "together aesthetic nuances, post modern experimentation, pleasurable images of ethnicity, linguistic play, humor, and new points of entry into history to create a compelling family saga that offers readers many sites of identification." She went on to claim that "[t]he novel marks Cisneros's definitive entry into the U.S.' literary canon." It was selected as Notable Book of the Year by the *New York Times*, the *Los Angeles Times*, the *San Francisco Chronicle*, the *Chicago Tribune*, and the *Seattle Times*.

During the twenty-first century, Cisneros has gained greater recognition for her writings, and she has a wider audience. All three of her works of fiction have been published in Spanish: *The House on Mango Street* in 1995,

Hollering Creek and Other Stories in 1996, and *Caramelo* in 2002. In addition, some of her pieces have been included in major literature anthologies, and a compilation of selections from her writings, *Vintage Cisneros*, was published in 2003. Cisneros has continued to be honored for her many achievements. Her alma mater, Loyola University, presented her an honorary Doctor of Humane Letters degree in 2002, and she was awarded the Texas Medal of the Arts in 2003. Two years later *Caramelo* won the Premio Napoli, and it was short-listed for the Dublin International IMPAC Award and nominated for the Orange Prize in England.

Although Cisneros has achieved national and international fame with her writings, she has not forgotten her humble roots, and she continues serving her community and helping other minority writers achieve their goals, using her position as a well-known writer to promote Chicana feminism. One example of Cisneros's attempts to help minority writers occurred in September 2006 when Cisneros was the featured speaker at the University of Michigan, Ann Arbor, during Hispanic Heritage Month. She taught minority students how they could become good writers by carefully explaining her prewriting, writing, and editing methods.

Before she begins writing, Cisneros says, "I usually meditate and I call my spirit allies—anyone in the spirit world that I've got connections with" and asks for humility and courage as she writes. Then she starts "writing in the language you would use if you were wearing your pajamas and you were seated at a table with your very good friend." After producing a rough draft, she edits by imagining "your enemy is seated on the other side of the table. . . . And your enemy is going to read

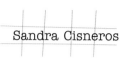

that with a viciousness. . . . He's going to shake it and really aim for that jugular. So you are going to polish, and revise, and rewrite, and cut out, and shape it, so that your enemy has no place to grip it. That's how you revise."

In 2006, Cisneros founded and became president of the Macondo Foundation, an organization of artists whose basic focus is to help other writers become successful. Although it was officially incorporated in 2006, this foundation grew out of the Macondo Writing Workshop that Cisneros had begun in 1995. In 2007, she continued working as a social activist, hosting a three-day reunion of Los MacArturos in San Antonio, where she once again worked with people in the community to bring about needed changes. After her mother died on November 1, 2007, Cisneros established the Elvira Cordero Cisneros Award for the Macondo Foundation in 2008, an award given to talented writers who are committed to their work and dedicated to nurturing the creativity of others. Cisneros is also the writer-in-residence at Our Lady of the Lake University in San Antonio.

Besides working for others in the first decade of the twenty-first century, Cisneros has continued to promote her own writing. Since 2009 marked the twenty-fifth anniversary of the publication of *The House on Mango Street*, Cisneros traveled to twenty cities in the United States to celebrate the book with her readers. She is interested in making a movie of *Caramelo*, a work she feels "is very cinematic." And, of course, she continues to write new works. One is a book of vignettes she plans to title *Infinito*, which she describes as "a little book of erotica." This, Cisneros claims, will be "a book that's for me because *Caramelo* was for my father and for the immigrants. *Woman Hollering* was for the community. *House on Mango Street* was for my students. This book is for me. And I haven't written a book of fiction that is for me." She is also working on a children's book called *Bravo, Bruno* and a book about writing titled *Working in My Pajamas*. This book title came about as a result of a seminar Cisneros and her friend Ruth Behar held with students at the University of Michigan in 2006 to talk about Cisneros's writing techniques. Cisneros suggested that both women dress in pajamas while they "talked in public about the things the two of us talked about on the phone late at night."

In October 2012, Cisneros published *Have You Seen Marie?*, a book she describes as a "fable for grown-ups." The book is a tale of grief and loss inspired by the death of Cisneros's mother. The author's goal in writing the book was to "help other people that are in pain from a death" and writing the story helped Cisneros "feel transformed by [her] mother's death, to feel her presence rather than her absence." The book is illustrated by Ester Hernandez, an artist best known for pastels and prints depicting Chicana and Latina women.

Cisneros still makes her home in her beloved house in San Antonio, which is no longer purple but bright Mexican pink. In her backyard is an office that she built in 2007 and painted "Mexican marigold on the outside, morning-glory violet on the inside." The cigar-smoking author shares her house with "yappy dogs, kamikaze cats, one lovesick parrot with a crush on me." Here she continues to live an independent life as a writer while serving her community.

SANDRA CISNEROS

25TH ANNIVERSARY EDITION

THE HOUSE ON MANGO STREET

The House on Mango Street is so beloved that it has been reprinted many times. In 2009, her publisher brought out a twenty-fifth anniversary edition.

THE HOUSE ON MANGO STREET

THE HOUSE ON MANGO STREET, Cisneros's most beloved and most critically acclaimed book, consists of a series of forty-four vignettes that loosely join together to form a novel about a Mexican-American girl, Esperanza Cordero. In spite of poverty and oppression, she dreams of and finds her way to an independent and fulfilling life.

The Story

Esperanza begins telling her story shortly after the Cordero family—"Mama, Papa, Carlos, Kiki, my sister Nenny, and me"—moves into a new house on Mango Street, the first one the family has owned. She is disappointed that it is an ugly, run-down building, not the type of place her parents had dreamed of buying.

Soon Esperanza meets neighbors who are about her age: Cathy, a friend for a few days before she moves out of the neighborhood; boys named Tito, Meme Ortiz, and Louie; and Lucy and Rachel, sisters who become Esperanza's good friends. The three girls buy a bike together, jump rope,

make up rhymes, look at clouds, argue, and play dress-up in high heels.

Esperanza also pays heed to other people in her neighborhood. There are Louie's cousins: a young man who steals a fancy car but gives the neighborhood kids a ride before he is arrested, and a boy-crazy girl named Marin, who meets a guy at a dance and mourns when he is killed by a hit-and-run driver. Esperanza describes the wild Vargas kids, whose father deserted them, and ambitious Alicia, who takes classes at the university, studies at night, and keeps house for her father and siblings. She observes two unusual adults: Ruthie, who lives with her mother, and Earl, a jukebox repairman who brings various women home with him. Esperanza also reveals that she is somewhat interested in Sire, a boy who sometimes stares at her.

Besides describing other people, Esperanza talks about herself. She begs her mother to let her eat lunch at school, but when she is allowed to do so, she does not enjoy herself because a nun scolded her and her food had turned greasy and cold. At another time she goes to her cousin's baptism, where she is miserable because she is wearing ugly school shoes, but when her uncle dances with her, she forgets about them. She tells about the death of her Mexican grandfather and her aunt Lupe. And she relates that she goes to a fortune-teller who tells her that she will have "a home in the heart."

Nearly a teenager, Esperanza is interested in her sexuality and romance. However, she realizes that her illusions of love are wrong when an old man lewdly kisses her. She also understands that the dreams of romance and a "happy-ever-after" life held by many of the women in her barrio are false ideals. She observes Ruthie, who has been deserted by her husband and seems to have lost her mind; she describes *Mamacita*, a homesick Mexican woman who cannot find happiness with her husband in a foreign country; she sees young Rafaela, who is so beautiful that her husband locks her in their apartment when he goes out with the guys; she witnesses the abuse Sally suffers from her father, who beats her because she is too beautiful; and she watches helplessly as Minerva, a young wife with two children, is beaten by her husband.

Esperanza and Sally become closer friends, playing together in an overgrown, deserted garden. But soon Sally prefers to flirt with the boys, and Esperanza becomes embarrassed when she tries to rescue Sally from them. When the two girls go to a carnival, Sally leaves with a boy, and Esperanza, waiting for her to return, is sexually assaulted by a stranger. Shortly after this, Sally marries a young man who, like Rafaela's husband, never lets her leave their house.

By the end of the novel, Esperanza has been told by three sisters that she is special and that she must help those who cannot get out when she leaves Mango Street. Her friend Alicia tells her the same thing: she cannot cut her ties to her community on Mango Street. Esperanza takes their words seriously. She vows to leave Mango Street and live in a house of her own where she will be independent, while, at the same time, she decides that she will write about Mango Street, which will be her way of coming back for the people who cannot leave.

Themes

This book is a coming-of-age story about a young girl's attempts to become the person she wants to be when there are no role models available to her as a poor, Mexican-American female. As a girl in the border zone between childhood and adulthood, Esperanza is trying to decide what direction her life should take, and she "struggles between what she is and what she would like to be." There are three primary issues that Cisneros examines: the problems of being a female in a patriarchal society; the conflict between pursuing the life of the mind and the traditional life of marriage and family; and the tension between individual identity and communal identity. She uses these themes to explore "the search for the real self and cultural responsibility in the face of different oppressions."

The Problems Facing Females in a Patriarchal Society

Throughout the book, Cisneros illustrates the difficulties of being a female in a Mexican-American community with its patriarchal attitudes, including the beliefs that a woman's place is in the home, that women are the possessions of men, and that men should have privileges and powers that are denied to women. Because of their low status, many women in Esperanza's culture are unhappy, worn-out, or abused. Some are sad because they are forced into subservient, domestic roles. Esperanza's own great-grandmother, who was "so wild she wouldn't marry," was compelled to become tame and servile when Esperanza's "great-grandfather threw a sack over her head and carried her off . . . as if she were a fancy chandelier." She remained an unhappy woman for the rest of her life because she "couldn't be all the things she wanted to be." Likewise, Esperanza's mother is worn-out and unhappy, spending her life working for her family instead of developing her talents. She "sighs" as she cooks, "I could've been somebody, you know? . . . I had brains. . . . I was a smart cookie then."

Although Esperanza's relatives are unhappy because they do not get to fulfill their dreams, other women are miserable because they are exploited or abused by the men of the community. Esperanza experiences male sexual exploitation firsthand when she is kissed on the mouth by an old, male coworker in "The First Job" and sexually assaulted in "Red Clowns." Many women are abused by family members, including Sally and Minerva, who are physically beaten by the men in their lives, and Rafaela and Sally, who are emotionally battered by their controlling husbands.

Like her great-grandmother and mother, Esperanza is fiercely independent and does not want to remain a second-class citizen living in a patriarchal community.

The Conflict Between Pursuing Independence and Marriage

Esperanza recognizes that married women living in the barrio are not free to pursue the life of the mind because they become trapped once they marry. Some are physically imprisoned. Rafaela's and Sally's husbands see their wives as possessions, useful when they want them and locked in safe places when they do not. Some women are condemned to hard lives because their husbands have deserted them:

By using the example of Cio-Cio San in *Madama Butterfly*, Esperanza's mother helps her daughter realize that the pursuit of the life of the mind is far more fulfilling and less dangerous than the pursuit of a "Prince Charming."

Rose Vargas is left alone to raise a multitude of children, and Ruthie wanders aimlessly and mindlessly in the barrio. Some, like Minerva, are trapped because they cannot go against their culture's expectations that women are supposed to silently tolerate abusive men. Therefore, even though her husband beats her, begs for forgiveness, and beats her again, Minerva does not leave him.

Some, like *Mamacita*, are trapped by loneliness. In comparison to many men, *Mamacita*'s husband is a good person: he does not imprison, abuse, or abandon his wife. In fact, he provides for her and their son. But *Mamacita*, forced to live where her husband chooses, is isolated and alienated, living in a foreign country whose people speak a language she does not understand. She is so separated from others in the barrio that Esperanza does not know the woman's real name. She is merely *Mamacita*, or "little mama." As Esperanza is trying to decide how she should live her life, she clearly understands "which route [she] didn't want to take—Sally, Rafaela, Ruthie, women whose lives were white crosses on the roadside," as Cisneros explains in the introduction to the novel.

Esperanza's mother is very influential in helping her daughter understand that she should pursue the life of the mind. Mrs. Cordero, a very talented woman who "can speak two languages," "sing an opera," "knows how to fix a T.V.," and "used to draw," has wasted her talents. As a high school dropout and now a wife and mother, she has turned her talents into mere hobbies: she embroiders flowers and sings in the kitchen. She urges her daughter to "go to school. Study hard," so that she can be an independent woman who fulfills her dreams.

Mrs. Cordero tries to reinforce her point by mentioning a fictional character. In the opera *Madama Butterfly*, a Japanese woman falls in love with a U.S. naval officer who is temporarily stationed in Japan, has his child after he leaves, and passively waits for him to return to marry her and make her life happy. When he does come back and informs her that he has married an American woman, Madama Butterfly's life is ruined. Esperanza's mother is clear: Esperanza must use her talents to make a life for herself and not depend on a man to make her life fulfilling and happy.

As a result of her mother's words and her own observations, Esperanza recognizes that the barrio women who have chosen the traditional roles of females have lost their freedom and individuality. Not wanting this type of life for herself, she claims the life of the mind. She will not marry and spend her time serving others. Instead, Esperanza will live alone and write.

The Tension Between Individual Identity and Communal Identity

Although Esperanza identifies herself with her family and community, she longs to become an independent individual. Critic Jacqueline Doyle calls this struggle the "tensions between belonging and not belonging," a conflict that is apparent in the opening chapters. Esperanza clearly has a sense of belonging to a particular family and a specific community while, at the same time, she does not want to belong to them. For example, she loves her family, but their house represents the opposite of what she wants to be. These contradictory feelings continue in "My Name" as Esperanza compares her name in Spanish and English. It sounds beautiful in Spanish but harsh in English. On the other hand, it has a positive connotation in English, "hope," and negative ones in Spanish, "waiting" and "sadness"; it also reminds her of Mexican "songs like sobbing." Furthermore, in her community, her name is common "like the number nine" and lacks beauty since it is a "muddy color," implying that she is an ordinary girl. Because Esperanza wants to be extraordinary, she says, "I would like to baptize myself under a new name, a name more like the real me, the one nobody sees. Esperanza as Lisandra or Maritza or Zeze the X. Yes. Something like Zeze the X will do."

She would like this unusual name because, as critic Anna Marie Sandoval points out, "Neither her culture nor her family would be able to define a name like 'Zeze the X.' She does not want a name associated with generations of women suffering as quiet rebels, sitting by the window, their anger silenced." Even though most of the things she notes about her community seem negative to Esperanza, she still recognizes that she does belong to the Mexican-American culture. After all, she is named for her independent Mexican great-grandmother. Esperanza, then, is pulled in two directions, identifying herself with both her Mexican-American community and her independent self.

By the end of the book, Esperanza resolves the struggle. Although she is "a girl who didn't want to belong," she has come to understand that she belongs to her community and has a responsibility to her people. At the same time, she will not allow herself to be trapped by her community or enslaved by its men. Therefore, Esperanza realizes that she must, for the sake of her freedom and happiness, leave Mango Street and "the house I belong but do not belong to" but never "forget who I am or where I come from." Critic Sonia Saldívar-Hull calls this an "act of resistance" in which "Esperanza comes to the conclusion that education will perhaps break the bondage of ignorance, exploitation, and domination for Mango Street women." Esperanza escapes by leaving the barrio to become a writer who will "speak for herself and her people, in her own voice. . . . She will speak in two tongues, English and Spanish, from inside and outside the barrio. She will speak for the nameless, . . . for the speechless, . . . for all women shut in their rooms, . . . for the dead, . . . [and] for herself."

By turning to writing for empowerment, Esperanza "has rewritten for herself a home where she will have the freedom to tell her story outside of the confines of a patriarchal culture. Her ultimate decision to return to her community with new educational tools demonstrates her commitment to creating new liberating places not only for herself but also for her community." *The House on Mango Street*, then, is the story of a girl who learns "both to accept and to alter her inheritance." As a result, she gains both belonging and freedom.

Analysis
Structure

Esperanza's story is told in chronological order over a one-year and one-summer period of time. At the end of the novel, Esperanza states that she has lived on Mango Street for one year and that her classmate Sally is not yet in eighth grade. Therefore, the novel begins during the summer before Esperanza enters seventh grade, when her family moves to the house on Mango Street. The chapters "The House on Mango Street" through "There Was an Old Woman She Had So Many Children She Didn't Know What to Do" occur during this summer when Esperanza gets acquainted with the neighborhood. The chapters "Alicia Who Sees Mice" through "Hips" take place during her seventh-grade school year. The chapters "The First Job" to the end of the novel relate to events taking place during the summer after seventh grade.

Cisneros encloses the forty-four vignettes with a frame in which Esperanza describes two houses. One is the physical house of poverty on Mango Street; the other is the imagined house of the promise of a better life. As part of this frame, Cisneros writes identical sentences in the first and last chapters: "We didn't always live on Mango Street. Before that we lived on Loomis on the third floor, and before that we lived on Keeler. Before Keeler it was Paulina. . . ."

Within this frame, the chapters are loosely connected. However, critic Maria Elena de Valdes thinks that the book has "a subtle sequential order to the short stories" in which Cisneros first describes the house and the narrator's views of it. Then she tells about Esperanza's family. From there she branches out to the neighborhood, interspersing the chapters about her world with reflective chapters about herself. These include "My Name," "Chanclas," "Elenita, Cards, Palm, Water," "Four Skinny Trees," "Bums in the Attic," "Beautiful and Cruel," "The Monkey Garden," "The Three Sisters," and "A House of My Own." Cisneros ends her novel with the "anticipated departure from the house and the literary return to it through writing."

Voice and Style

Cisneros uses the first-person point of view and a stream-of-consciousness technique to tell the story of Esperanza. Readers see everything through Esperanza's eyes as she describes what she sees, feels, and thinks. Cisneros makes her narrator seem like a young girl by selecting simple, everyday words mixed with some slang and a few Spanish words, and by writing in short sentences and even in sentence fragments. Esperanza's language becomes more vivid by Cisneros's use of similes (comparisons using *like* and *as*) and metaphors (comparisons without using *like* or *as*). For example, at the end of "Boys & Girls," Esperanza's comparison of herself to "a red balloon, a balloon tied to an anchor" colorfully portrays her view of herself: that she is different from other people but that she cannot fulfill her dream of flight out of the neighborhood because she is held back by her young age and her family. In the following chapter, "My Name," Esperanza talks about her name in metaphors, calling it a "muddy color" and "the Mexican records my father plays on Sunday morning when he is shaving." The use of similes and metaphors continues throughout the book, reaching a climax near the end of the novel when Alicia tells Esperanza, "Like it or not you are Mango Street." Through this metaphor, Esperanza begins to realize that she cannot deny her heritage without negating herself.

Characters

Esperanza

According to Dr. Nicholas Sloboda, professor of multiethnic American literature, the main character of the novel, Esperanza, is "a vital and dynamic individual" who, in spite of "the harsh socioeconomic realities around her," maintains "her personal dreams and playful spirit." She is a child who enjoys playing with other children, particularly Rachel and Lucy, but, like many children, she is painfully shy around people she does not know well. For example, in "The First Job" and "A Rice Sandwich," she is too bashful to eat with coworkers and fellow students. She is also childlike in her trusting nature. In fact, it is because she trusts Sally to meet her at the carnival that she waits alone in the dark and is sexually assaulted in "Red Clowns."

Esperanza is both shy and bold, confident that her sister will be happy to be part-owner of the bicycle shown here as part of the action in the Steppenwolf Theatre company's dramatization of Cisneros's book.

Although Esperanza is a typical young woman in many ways, she is also a unique, strong individual. She is an independent girl who dares to take Nenny's savings without asking her, confident that her sister will be glad to be part-owner of a bicycle. She is also an intelligent and creative individual who writes poetry, describes her experiences and feelings with similes and metaphors, and corrects Lucy's grammar. Because of her intelligence, Esperanza recognizes that traditional female behaviors and roles are traps. Therefore, she rejects the lifestyles of Rafaela, Minerva,

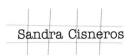
Mamacita, Rose Vargas, Sally, and Marin, realizing that these females have allowed themselves to become victims. Esperanza, instead, chooses to be "beautiful" and "cruel" so she can keep power for herself.

By the end of the novel, she wisely decides to use her creativity to forge her own identity. At the same time, she realizes that her writings cannot be separated from her community because she will "always be Esperanza" and "always be Mango Street." Therefore, she resolves to be the "somebody" who "makes [the Latino community] better."

Professor Sloboda sums up Esperanza's character: "With her protagonist exhibiting an enthusiasm and vigor for life, Cisneros shows how Esperanza learns to use this energy to build a will within herself. . . . [S]he comes to accept her past and, at the same time, transform her present. By developing this strength of character, Esperanza finds herself able to move beyond assigned, contained, and disempowered mental and physical ghettoes, and live a meaningful and fulfilling life."

Sally

Esperanza's classmate and friend Sally is a very attractive girl whose father beats her because her "sexuality is doubly threatening to her father's masculinity. Not only could she betray him by being promiscuous, but her beauty might also entice a man to violate her." To escape her father's assaults, Sally marries before she enters eighth grade and seems to fulfill her dreams since she has a husband and her own house. But her happiness is as artificial as the roses on her linoleum floor and the "wedding cake" ceiling in her house.

She remains in her house with its beautiful contents, unable to leave because her jealous and controlling husband does not permit her to go out. Although "Sally gains material wealth, she loses her autonomy, character, and perhaps most important, her dignity."

Alicia

Alicia, a girl a little older than Esperanza, is a role model for her. Alicia's father is a traditional Latino who believes that since his wife is dead, his daughter should be responsible for all the housework. Alicia fulfills his expectations, caring for her younger siblings in the family's run-down apartment. But she does not allow this work to drive away her own ambitions. Rejecting the traditional passive role for women, Alicia studies at night and attends college so she can become an independent person. She also understands and accepts a person's responsibilities to a community and encourages Esperanza to be a free woman without rejecting her culture.

Symbols

Symbols are tangible items such as objects or people that stand for abstract ideas or thoughts. In *The House on Mango Street*, Cisneros uses three primary symbols—a house, four skinny trees, and the monkey garden—to help develop her themes and her characters.

House

Two houses, the home of the Cordero family and the house of Esperanza's dreams, not only provide the framework for the story but also operate on a symbolic level to show Esperanza's dreams of self-fulfillment. There are four main vignettes—the first chapter and the last three chapters of the novel—in which the house on Mango Street is compared to Esperanza's dream house.

In chapter one, the physical house on Mango Street is "a sign—at once real and symbolic—of the rift between the reality and the dreams of Esperanza." Esperanza loathes her ramshackle home because it is "small and red with tight steps in front and windows so small you'd think they were holding their breath." Her family's poverty, exemplified by the ugly house, threatens to destroy Esperanza's dreams of self-fulfillment. Therefore, she desires a "real house," one that reflects her worth as a human being.

In the last three chapters, Esperanza not only realizes that she can escape her impoverished life through her imagination but also learns that she cannot reject her Mango Street house. Alicia is the first one to help educate Esperanza about her relationship with her house, her poverty, and her culture. In "Alicia & I Talking on Edna's Steps," after Esperanza insists that the house on Mango Street "isn't my house . . . I don't belong . . . I never had a house . . . only one I dream of," Alicia patiently but forcefully explains that Esperanza is a part of this house because she is a part of its culture.

Not convinced by Alicia's messages, Esperanza, in "A House of My Own," describes the physical house she will have someday, a place that will give her identity as a female Mexican-American writer. She begins by describing what it cannot be: "Not a flat. Not an apartment in back. Not a man's house. Not a daddy's." Instead, her place will be a "house all my own" that holds only her personal items: "my porch and my pillow, my pretty purple petunias. My books and my stories. My two shoes waiting beside the bed." This "quiet as snow" house, where there is "nobody to shake a stick at. Nobody's garbage to pick up after," will be her personal space. Here she will live an independent and creative life as a respected member of American society.

In the last chapter, "Mango Says Goodbye Sometimes," Esperanza focuses on her sense of herself as a writer and as a member of the community destined to return to "those who cannot out." She accepts the idea that her house gives her freedom to be herself and yet she belongs to Mango Street.

Four Skinny Trees

In "Four Skinny Trees," Esperanza uses the four small trees that have grown in spite of the city's concrete side-walks to symbolize herself and her future life. She is not only physically similar to the trees with "skinny necks and pointy elbows" but also emotionally like them because she too is strong and keeps trying to survive. Esperanza claims that the trees possess "strength," sending "ferocious roots beneath the ground," and they "grab the earth" and "bite the sky" and "never quit their anger" in order to survive in a hostile environment. Like these "[f]our raggedy excuses" "who do not belong here but are here," Esperanza vows to strive to overcome the obstacles she faces as a Mexican-American girl living in a run-down neighborhood of Chicago where she feels she does not belong.

The Monkey Garden

The monkey garden is a symbol for the loss of innocence. Like the biblical Garden of Eden, it is filled with lush vegetation and animal life: "sunflowers big as flowers on Mars," "thick cockscombs," "dizzy bees and bow-tied fruit flies turning somersaults and humming in the air," "sweet peach trees," "thorn roses and thistle and pears," "big green apples hard as knees," and "the sleepy smell of rotting wood, damp earth and dusty hollyhocks thick and perfumy." But it is made into a junkyard where people abandon their worn-out vehicles.

Nevertheless, the children of the barrio find it a magical playground, a place in which Esperanza has fun being a child even though she recognizes that she is maturing: "Who was it that said I was getting too old to play the games? . . . I only remember that when the others ran, I wanted to run too, up and down and through the monkey garden, fast as the boys."

But one day she is forced to grow up. Not understanding that Sally is flirting with Tito and his friends when she goes into the garden to kiss them, Esperanza tries to save her and feels like a fool when Sally and the boys tell her to "go home" and "leave us alone." As she hides at the end of the garden—like Eve when she is cast out of Eden—Esperanza wants to die. She has lost her childhood innocence, and "the garden that had been such a good place to play didn't seem mine" any longer.

Motifs

Motifs are recurring elements that help develop the themes of the novel. There are three predominant motifs that Cisneros uses in this novel: fairy tales, a woman at a window leaning on her elbow, and shoes and feet.

Fairy Tales

The fairy-tale motif helps develop Cisneros's theme of females being imprisoned in a patriarchal society. In particular, the fairy-tale motif shows the difference between the real lives of women in the barrio and the romantic dreams of women who think they will live "happily ever after" as soon as they find "Prince Charming."

The most prominent fairy tale used by Cisneros is "Cinderella," which she introduces in "The Family of Little Feet." Esperanza describes her elation when she and her friends are given high heels: "Hurray! Today we are Cinderella because our feet fit exactly." But instead of finding happiness, the girls' "encounters with men as they strut in their glass slippers escalate in danger until they flee from the drunken 'bum man,' a leering Prince Charming whose kiss they refuse."

Throughout the book, Cisneros shows that the women of Mango Street are types of Cinderellas. As critic Michelle Scalise Sugiyama explains, "Like Cinderella, the women of Mango Street are confined to a life of domestic drudgery. Like Cinderella, their suitability as wives is symbolically determined by their shoes and feet. Like Cinderella, they use their sexuality to acquire a husband who they think will take them far, far away where they will live happily ever after. And like Cinderella, the women of Mango Street do not see this escape is a trap."

Young Marin is a type of Cinderella, trapped in a house doing domestic chores. Like Cinderella, Marin wants to have beautiful clothes so "Prince Charming" will see her, marry her, and change her life. Therefore, she longs to work downtown "since you always get to look beautiful and get to wear nice clothes and can meet someone in the subway who might marry you and take you to live in a big house far away." But no Prince Charming comes for Marin, and she is sent back to Puerto Rico.

A second fairy tale used by Cisneros is "Rapunzel," the story of a princess locked in a high tower who lets down her long golden hair so that Prince Charming can climb up the wall to rescue her. However, Cisneros changes the story so that the beautiful young woman is imprisoned, not rescued, by Prince Charming. When Rafaela's husband locks her indoors so she won't run away when he is away with his friends, she leans out the window and "dreams her hair is like Rapunzel's" so she can be rescued. Even though she understands the terrible truth—that her Prince Charming is her jailer—she still waits for someone or something else to come to bring her happiness.

Those women who do get married often find that their Prince Charmings either disappear or disappoint them. Rosa Vargas's husband abandoned her and their children. Ruthie's husband is also not seen. Esperanza's godmothers' husbands have died or left. Minerva's husband leaves, returns, beats her, and leaves again so that, instead of living "happily ever after," Minerva is "always sad like a house on fire." Sally, like Rafaela, has been imprisoned by her Prince Charming.

Through these fairy tales, Cisneros shows that Esperanza's view of love after she is sexually assaulted is accurate: "They all lied. All the books and magazines, everything that told it wrong" because when a man says, "I love, I love you, Spanish girl," the reality is "dirty fingernails against my skin" and a "sour smell." Esperanza knows that love does not bring a Prince Charming who makes a woman live happily ever after.

A Woman at a Window Leaning on Her Elbow

Cisneros creates the illusion of women becoming prisoners in their homes by providing multiple images of females inside houses sadly looking out of windows and doors while waiting for someone or something to change their lives. She shows that homes for Mexican-American women are not places of freedom but prisons because men control the domestic spaces. The first person Esperanza describes as caged in her home is her great-grandmother, who, after she was forced to marry, "looked out the window her whole life, the way so many women sit their sadness on an elbow." Esperanza, acknowledging that she has inherited her name, notes: "I don't want to inherit her place by the window."

Throughout the novel, Cisneros includes other women who longingly look out of their prison homes. Marin "can't come out" but "stands in the doorway a lot" waiting for some man to rescue her. Beautiful Rafaela leans out the window begging the neighborhood children to bring her sweet drinks. She "wishes there were sweeter drinks, not bitter like an empty room, but sweet sweet like the island, like the dance hall down the street where women much older than her throw green eyes easily like dice and open homes with keys." *Mamacita*, homesick for Mexico, "sits all day by the window." And poor Sally might have the worst life because her husband not only beats her but "doesn't let her look out the window."

Shoes and Feet

Cisneros uses the motif of shoes and feet "to symbolize female sexuality" and show the dangers and confinements that come with adult femininity. This is seen explicitly in the chapter on high heels, "The Family of Little Feet." After Esperanza and her friends put on their newly acquired high heels, they immediately note that they have become sexually desirable, recognizing that "[w]e have legs" that are "good to look at, and long," and they practice how to "cross and uncross [their] legs." As they are "strutting" in their high heels, they realize their sexual power over men who "can't take their eyes off of [them]," and they are excited when a boy cries, "Ladies, lead me to heaven." The girls are also aware that less attractive women, "girls with the same fat

Long before *Sex and the City*, Cisneros used the motif of shoes to symbolize female sexuality. Unlike the popular TV show, Cisneros's story "The Family of Little Feet" points out the downside of high heels.

face," are jealous of them. But their exhilaration at being sexually desirable is short-lived. When a drunken bum solicits Rachel, they soon realize that adult women face great dangers. They also begin to understand "the threatening nature of male sexual power" when Mr. Benny chastises them, "Them shoes are dangerous," he says. "You girls too young to be wearing shoes like that. Take them shoes off before I call the cops." As critic Michelle Sealise Sugiyama points out, "The shoe motif and the use of violence by males to control female sexuality come together in the person of Mr. Benny, whose reaction to the high-heeled girls is, to say the least, extreme. . . . Mr. Benny's threat to summon the police confirms that control is indeed the issue: the police are agents of patriarchal power who use force (or threatened force) to control refractory members of society."

In contrast to the dangerous high heels, Cisneros uses homely school shoes in two chapters to show a lack of sexual desirability. In "Chanclas," Esperanza describes her feelings of being unattractive when she wears her old, clumsy school shoes, called *chanclas*, to a party. Because of her ugly shoes, Esperanza feels that her feet are "growing bigger and bigger . . . swell[ing] big and heavy like plungers," making her feel undesirable. In "The Monkey Garden," Esperanza's school shoes help visually portray her loss of the "Edenic innocence of her girlhood." After Sally kisses the boys, disillusioned Esperanza says, "I looked at my feet in their white socks and ugly round shoes," symbols of girlhood. "They seemed far away. They didn't seem to be my feet anymore." Now that she has been initiated into adulthood, she knows she will never play in the garden again.

In other chapters, Cisneros uses shoes and feet to show "images of constricting femininity." Rose Vargas in "There Was an Old Woman She Had So Many Children She Didn't Know What to Do" is like "the Mother Goose character who lived in a shoe." She has given up on her kids, who are "too many and too much." Fat *Mamacita* with "a tiny pink shoe, a foot soft as a rabbit's ear," and "a dozen boxes of satin high heels" uses her shoes for nothing because she never leaves her house. And Sire's girlfriend, Lois, is so dependent on men that she "can't tie her shoes."

Although Cisneros shows that sexually desirable women have small feet and pretty shoes, she makes it clear that female desirability leads to dangers and loss of freedom.

Reception

The House on Mango Street began as a relatively unknown work when it was first published in 1984 by Arte Público Press. But it came to be viewed as a literary masterpiece as early as 1985, when it received the Before Columbus Foundation's American Book Award. After it was reissued by Random House, a mainstream press, in 1991, Cisneros's first major work received national attention and gained a wide reading public. Critic Ellen McCracken describes this book as having "two lives to date: the first seven years, in which its launch by Arte Público in 1984 helped to inaugurate the long-awaited entrance of women fiction writers in the Chicano literary renaissance, and its second publication by Random House in 1991, after which it rapidly reached a vast national and international readership." McCracken goes on to explain that "[a]lthough the book was not well known and was difficult to obtain in its first stage, it quickly entered the literary canon once it was distributed more widely in the decade of flowering multiculturalism of the 1990s."

The "circumstances surrounding its seemingly meteoric rise within the US publishing industry" have been examined by critic Felicia J. Cruz, who notes that *The House on Mango Street* was first published in a year that "witnessed a revitalized interest in Chicana literature." Cisneros's publisher, Nicolás Kanellos, explains that Cisneros and a handful of other Chicana writers "inscribed themselves on the published page precisely at the time when literary publishing was . . . opening up to women as writers and intellectuals. It was this generation, very much aware of the business of writing, of the industry's networks, and of the norms of language, metaphor, and craft protected by the academy, that was able to break into commercial and intellectual circles and cause a stir."

Although Cisneros was lucky to be writing at a time when there was a demand for works written by female minority writers, her popularity was also due to her talents. In fact, she was identified as the best of the Chicana writers of the 1980s, "the standout among a group of writers that included Pat Mora, Evangelina Vigil, and Ana Castillo." As a result, Cisneros's book became a college campus standard by the late 1980s and early 1990s, often read in a variety of different academic disciplines, including American literature, women's studies, multicultural literature, creative writing, ethnic studies, sociology, and psychology.

Enthusiasm for the book has not died down. Critic Felicia J. Cruz notes that the "appeal of *Mango Street* clearly remains unabated in both the real and literary worlds," while teacher Carol Jago claims that it has been "enjoyed by readers of almost any age." Very young children enjoy the chapter "Hairs," which has been turned into a picture book. Many older readers see Cisneros's novel as a reflection of their lives and, as a result, respond personally and emotionally to Esperanza's quest for the American dream. Besides the emotional relationship to the book, readers, according to Cruz, also enjoy "its nonintellectual themes and its rebellious, colloquial, even antiliterary tone." A number of students appreciate that "the book offers a window through which to view the race-class-gender paradigm that characterizes the Latino experiences in the United States." On college campuses in the twenty-first century, students have "lavished enthusiastic praise on the book: some admired its lyrical, albeit 'simplistic' tone, while others related to the trials and tribulations of the novel's young female protagonist."

Not only is the book enjoyed by students and other readers, but it is also of interest to scholars, who have published numerous essays about it since the 1980s. It has won worldwide attention, having been translated into a variety of languages. In 2009, National Public Radio interviewer Bob Edwards reported that more than 4 million copies of *The House on Mango Street* had been sold. People around the globe enjoy reading about Esperanza, relating to her loneliness and her longings as they come to realize new possibilities for their lives.

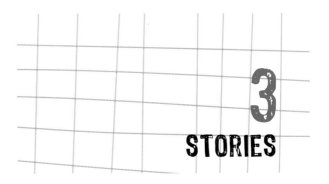

STORIES

ALTHOUGH HER SHORT FICTION has been published in various magazines, including *Glamour* and *Ms.*, Cisneros has published only one book of short stories, *Woman Hollering Creek and Other Stories*, which appeared in 1991. These twenty-two stories concern the lives of Mexican and Chicana women living in Texas, Chicago, and Mexico from the 1960s through the 1980s, with the exception of "Eyes of Zapata," which is set in the early twentieth century. The narrators are usually characters in the stories, ranging from a young preschool child to an old man. However, most of the narrators are women who suffer because of cultural expectations, solitude, and male aggression and dominance. Unlike *The House on Mango Street*, in which almost all the women remain trapped in their homes inside the barrio, "*Woman Hollering Creek* offers stories of a variety of women trying various means of escape, through resistance to traditional female socialization, through sexual and economic independence, self-fashioning, and feminist activism, as well as through fantasy, prayer, magic, and art."

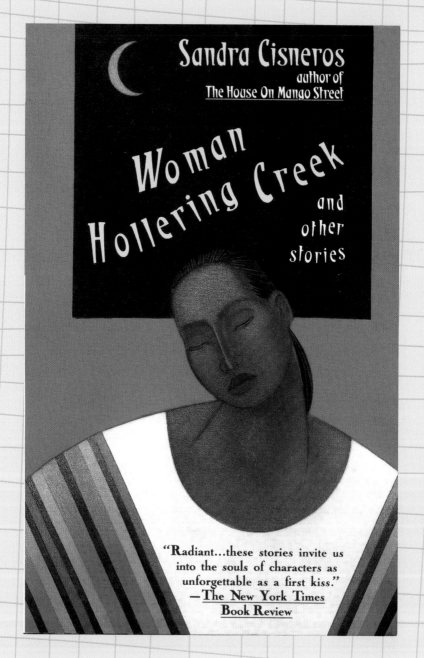

Woman Hollering Creek and Other Stories is Cisneros's only published book of stories.

The book is divided into three sections, each containing a story that has the same title as the section it is in. Although each story is complete in itself, "as whole sections they define specific areas of adversity—specifically feminine adversity . . . [caused by] a social structure that allows little cultural movement and less possibility for the formation of an identity outside the boundaries of the barrio." Cisneros begins with seven stories set during the childhood years in the section titled "My Lucy Friend Who Smells Like Corn." In these pieces, "girls seem secure in poor, but happy and warm homes, [although] there are some suggestions of gender restrictions." The two stories comprising the second section, "One Holy Night," are about adolescent females who encounter many types of dangers as they develop sexually, including seduction, abandonment, rape, and death. In the last section, "There Was a Man, There Was a Woman," Cisneros tells thirteen stories about adults, mostly women, moving "toward situations where women are attempting to free themselves from the world of sexual violence, stereotypes and controlled identity."

Three of Cisneros's popular stories about childhood are found in the first section: "Eleven," "Mexican Movies," and "Barbie-Q." The title story, "Woman Hollering Creek," is the first story of the third section.

"Eleven"

In "Eleven," Cisneros tells a heart-wrenching story about the difference between happy illusions and harsh reality. It is Rachel's eleventh birthday, a day that should be happy because

her family will celebrate: "There's a cake Mama's making for tonight, and when Papa comes home from work we'll eat it. There'll be candles and presents and everybody will sing Happy birthday, happy birthday to you, Rachel." But Rachel's birthday turns out to be one of the most miserable days of her young life because of something that happens at school.

Rachel begins by relating that the distress she suffers this day is made worse because she thinks she should be a mature eleven-year-old, but instead she is childlike because all her earlier ages are inside her body "like an onion or like the rings inside a tree trunk or like my little wooden dolls that fit one inside the other, each year inside the next one." Her terrible day starts when a girl mistakenly tells the teacher that a sweater Rachel finds repulsive belongs to Rachel, and the teacher places it on her desk. When the teacher later forces her to wear the ugly garment, Rachel begins crying out of embarrassment, shame, and disgust. Even though another girl later remembers that the sweater belongs to her, Rachel remains upset. She realizes that although her family will celebrate her birthday that evening, for her "it's too late." Rachel wishes that she were 102 years old so that this horrible day would be "far away already."

Cisneros evokes the senses to help readers experience the intense emotions of a girl who is eleven, while also still being "ten, nine, eight, seven, six, five, four, three, two, one." She makes readers see the repulsive sweater "with red plastic buttons and a collar and sleeves all stretched out like you could use it for a jump rope," smell its nauseating "cottage cheese" odor, and feel that it is "all itchy and full of germs that aren't even mine." Cisneros also helps readers participate in Rachel's humiliation by using vivid similes. For example, Rachel says she is trying not to cry even though she's "feeling sick inside, like the part of me that's three wants to come out of my eyes." When her tears finally do pour out, readers can experience the way her body feels: "my body shaking like when you have the hiccups, and my whole head hurts like when you drink milk too fast."

Although the story can be read simply as a tale of a young girl's embarrassment and humiliation when a teacher forces her to wear an ugly sweater, Cisneros portrays a disturbing theme as she shows "the difficulty of maintaining a unity of self in the face of authority." The pain and suffering Rachel endures when she is bullied into submitting to authority seem as if they might be the beginning of a lifetime of submission and loss of identity that Rachel's society expects for Mexican-American women.

"Mexican Movies"

On the surface, "Mexican Movies" seems to be a story about family contentment and happiness. The narrator is a young girl, probably six or seven years old, who tells about a typical Sunday evening in which she goes to a theater to watch a Mexican movie with her parents and little brother. She describes the types of romantic movies they watch; the theater's lobby, where she and her brother are sent during provocative love scenes; the activities she and her brother do during the movie; her mother sitting on her feet throughout the movie because of her fear of rats; and her feelings of contentment when she falls asleep and her parents carry her home and put her to bed.

In this film starring Pedro Infante, the hero comes to the rescue of the damsel in distress. In "Mexican Movies," Cisneros makes the point that this is far from real life.

However, as critic Jeff Thomson points out, Cisneros subtly uses satire to develop her themes of "stereotypes and enforced identity," showing that the Mexican movies are "stereotypes that limit their ability to be accepted in the white world." Cisneros contrasts the safe, contented world of the narrator with the false happiness of the Mexicans in movies such as "the films of Pedro Infante (his name itself denotes a childlike, false identity) who 'always sings riding a horse and wears a big sombrero and never tears the dresses off the ladies, and the ladies throw flowers from balconies and usually somebody dies, but not Pedro Infante because he has to sing the happy song at the end.'" Meanwhile, the real children, unaware of stereotypes, go happily about their lives, playing in the aisles, buying treats, sitting on the stage, and sleeping peacefully. At their young age, they do not need to become something they are not in order to find contentment.

"Barbie-Q"

"Barbie-Q" is another deceptively simple sketch about childhood activities. The narrator is a girl, probably about nine or ten, who is talking to a sister or friend about Barbie dolls. The narrator then tells about finding an assortment of smoke- and water-damaged dolls that are "Barbie's friends and relatives," a Ken doll, and Barbie outfits at a flea market. Although the dolls smell of smoke and one has a partially melted foot, the young girls are pleased to have new dolls and outfits.

Though Cisneros was not the first feminist to show the harm caused by female stereotypes like Barbie, her short story "Barbie-Q" is arguably one of her strongest, not least because it is also a comment on the tragedy of poverty in America.

In this story, Cisneros shows the harm caused by "artificial feminine stereotypes that are epitomized in every Barbie doll." The girls in this story are "seduced by the politics of the advertising industry with dreams of glamour, romance, and success embodied by Barbie, the American icon of feminine perfection. They internalize the promises of professional and romantic success that are supposed to come with the right wardrobe." At the same time, "[t]hey realize the capitalist version of feminine perfection is flawed at its foundation." This is clearly seen in Cisneros's biting conclusion of the sketch, in which the young narrator explains how women can cover up any flaws with beautiful clothes: "And if the prettiest doll, Barbie's MOD'ern cousin Francie with real eyelashes, eyelash brush included, has a left foot that's melted a little—so? If you dress her in her new 'Prom Pinks' outfit, satin splendor with matching coat, gold belt, clutch, and hair bow included, so long as you don't lift her dress, right?—who's to know." Cisneros here "is both attacking and acknowledging the depths our culture goes to in an attempt to hide women's assumed 'faults,'" writes Jeff Thomson.

This story can also be read as a comment on the reality of poverty. Since the narrator and her playmate play with cheap, damaged dolls, Cisneros shows "that some children are less equal than others in attaining this gendered version of the American Dream."

"Woman Hollering Creek"

In the title story of the book, Cisneros, using a third-person narrator, explores one way a woman can escape from a world of sexual violence, dependence, and entrapment. A young Mexican bride, Cleófilas, moves to Seguin, Texas, with her husband, Juan, believing that she will find the type of romantic love and marriage shown in the Mexican soap operas. She imagines she will be like the *telenovela* heroine Lucia Mendez, who believes that "to suffer for love is good. The pain all sweet somehow. In the end." In her new home Cleófilas encounters an entirely different world from the one pictured in the soap operas. "The reality of Seguin is Juan's modest job with a beer company, a dilapidated house, no *zocalo* (town square) to congregate in, and few female neighbors to provide the warm community bonds of the Mexican village."

When her husband becomes physically abusive, Cleófilas thinks about drowning herself and her baby son, identifying with the creek on their property, Woman Hollering Creek, which she thinks may be calling to her in the voice of La Llorona, the Weeping Woman from Mexican folklore who wails because she killed her children.

During Cleófilas's second pregnancy, a different means of escape becomes possible when a nurse discovers Cleófilas's bruised body and arranges for a friend to drive Cleófilas and her little boy to a bus station in San Antonio so they can return to Cleófilas's father's house in Mexico. When they cross Woman Hollering Creek, Cleófilas is astonished that her rescuer "opened her mouth and let out a yell as loud as any mariachi" and laughs. Cleófilas soon joins in, "gurgling" "a long ribbon of laughter like water." Thus, Cleófilas finds the strength to begin a new, happier life for herself and her children.

In this story, Cisneros examines three major themes. One is the idea that women think they are supposed to suffer for love. Cisneros develops this theme by "juxtapos[ing] the heroines of contemporary Mexican *telenovelas* with the traditional figure La Llorona to imply that then, now, and always the ideals of femininity that Mexican popular culture presents to its women are models of pain and suffering."

As the story opens, Cleófilas is a naive girl who thinks that soap operas reflect real life. Believing in a romantic world portrayed in the *telenovelas* in which women marry loving husbands, Cleófilas innocently marries a man she hardly knows but who seems to be an ideal husband: he lives in Seguin, Texas, a name that sounds lovely to her; he drives a pickup truck, implying that he has money; and he wants to marry her, offering her passion and romance. Her childlike innocence continues when she first crosses Woman Hollering Creek, which she regards as "so pretty and full of happily ever after."

Even after her husband beats her, Cleófilas still clings to her cultural beliefs "that suffering is inherent in romantic passion, and that this suffering is not only natural and expected but is a reasonable price to pay for being loved." This is the lesson she learned in the *telenovelas*: a woman must do "whatever one can . . . at whatever the cost" to find love, a lesson that prepared Cleófilas "for the submissions of a beaten wife."

Another theme Cisneros looks at is the ways in which women become silenced, marginalized, and alienated. Soon after moving to Seguin, Cleófilas realizes that she is alone. She "lives in isolation" and "characterizes Seguin in terms of her isolation and hopelessness." She shares no common traits with her violent, crude, selfish, boring husband, but, at the same time, she is totally dependent on him for food, shelter, and transportation. He cuts off all her ties to Mexico by refusing to let her write or phone her family. She is isolated from her community because she speaks no English. She has no friends. Cleófilas cannot confide in her two neighbors who live with their own troubles: Delores, meaning "sorrow," lives with the memory of her dead husband and sons, while Soledad, meaning "loneliness," is alone because her "husband had either died, or run away with an ice-house floozie, or simply gone out for cigarettes one afternoon and never came back." Cisneros, then, shows that men, women, and the Mexican-American community work together to silence and marginalize women.

A third theme she explores is the culture's relegation of women to passive, subservient roles while tolerating male privilege and aggression. As time passes in Seguin, Cleófilas's romantic dreams that women are supposed to passively suffer for love slowly disappear as she experiences her husband's violence. She is further disillusioned with male privilege and aggression when she hears the "foul-smelling fool" Maximiliano make a coarse joke about her and begins to understand that men feel that they own women.

His idea of ownership is even more apparent to Cleófilas as she reflects that Maximiliano "killed his wife in an ice-house brawl when she came at him with a mop. I had to shoot, he had said—she was armed." The townspeople obviously tolerated his aggression and murder, for nothing happened to him. Cleófilas recognizes that male aggression is widespread, not only in her community but also in her culture: "This woman found on the side of the interstate. This one pushed from a moving car. This one's cadaver, this one unconscious, this one beaten blue. Her ex-husband, her husband, her lover, her father, her brother, her uncle, her friend, her coworker. Always. The same grisly news in the pages of the dailies." Although her husband calls her fears of male violence "exaggerations," Cleófilas "comes to realize that her own culture has duped her, luring her into marriage with idealized romantic stories while simultaneously elevating her husband to a position of power that Cisneros describes in biblical terms: 'this man, this father, this rival, this keeper, this lord, this master, this husband till kingdom come.'"

As Cleófilas becomes more and more despondent in her passive, subservient role, while her husband continues his violence toward her, she looks for a means to escape and finds three possible avenues: the creek, the border, and the *telenovelas*. All of these "offer her different escape fantasies: homicide and/or suicide, like La Llorona; dramatic border crossings, like the escape of an outlaw desperado from the U.S. into Mexico, or the crossing of *mojados* and smuggler *coyotes*; or *telenovelas*, soap operas that provide the escape of entertainment." After she rejects the *telenovelas*, Cleófilas dwells on escaping by drowning herself and her baby in the creek.

However, by the end of the story, Cleófilas finds a better way of leaving her violent husband by receiving help from Graciela (grace) and Felice (happiness) to return to Mexico. Although Cleófilas continues to play the role of a subservient wife to her husband by promising him that she will not tell anyone about his beatings, she actively takes measures to save herself and her child: she gets her husband to drive her to the doctor for a prenatal checkup; she lets her bruised body tell the story of her husband's assaults; she saves money to buy bus tickets; and she arranges to go with a stranger to San Antonio to catch the bus to Mexico. Thus, Cleófilas goes against the cultural norms and leaves her husband, defying "both the church and her community, which define leaving one's husband as a sin. . . . [But] Cisneros's story redefines sin, locating it in Cleófilas's abusive husband and the culture that excuses his violence, in the neighbor women who fail to recognize her plight and protect her, and in the community that leaves her isolated and dependent on her abuser." By leaving her husband, Cleófilas becomes a stronger, less passive woman.

In the title story, "Woman Hollering Creek," Cleofilas learns about the power of women—when they help one another rather than passively relying on men to help or hurt them.

Not only has Cleófilas begun to take charge of her own life, but, through Felice, she also finds a new way of viewing women's role in society. She recognizes that Felice, "[h]aving rejected the cultural message that she is nothing without a man . . . has saved herself from a life of silence, isolation, and dependence." Furthermore, she sees that Felice "appropriates for women the privileges of freedom and mobility [symbolized by Felice's pickup truck] usually associated with masculinity."

When Cleófilas hears Felice's yell as they cross Woman Hollering Creek, she reinterprets the meaning of the creek, the main symbol in the story. Throughout the story, Cleófilas assumes that a woman must be passive and, therefore, must be hollering from "[p]ain or rage." The Spanish name for the creek, La Gritona, which means "hollering or yelling woman," reminds Cleófilas of a sad figure in Mexican folklore: La Llorona, the Weeping or Wailing Woman. According to critic Jean Wyatt, there are different versions of the La Llorona legend, but all of them contain the idea of La Llorona's wailing sound. In one legend, "she kills her three children because they get in the way of her wild living; after her own death, God sends her back to seek them eternally."

In other legends, La Llorona becomes combined with Cortez's lover, La Malinche. She is sometimes seen as a victim of Cortez, a mother who "killed the son, then herself, rather than be separated from her child" when "Cortez wanted to take their son back to Spain with him." However, at other times, she is regarded as a traitor to her people, who mourns the dead Indian children she betrayed to Cortez. Still another legend views La Llorona as a woman who foresaw the conquest by Cortez and cries for "the Indians about to be slaughtered, and her cry continues through the centuries to mourn the loss of the indigenous civilization." No matter which legend is followed, La Llorona often "appears by the shore of a river or lake—she is said to have drowned her children—and sometimes she acts as siren, enticing men into the water to die." The one consistent idea of the La Llorona legend is that she cries in sorrow. Cisneros transforms all of these versions, making La Llorona "powerful and active—rather than suffering and passive." She becomes "a female figure whose cry is not a feeble weeping but a *grito*, a yell or shout signifying womanly strength and joy in that strength."

With her new knowledge about a woman's ability to be free and independent, Cleófilas begins to laugh. Although she is returning to her father's house and is tied down by two children, she has the possibility of living a happy life because she has learned that a woman does not have to remain passive and holler only out of anger or pain—she can control her life and holler for sheer joy. Therefore, "Cleófilas's laugh at the ending of the story becomes her own *grito* in independence." She has learned "that she must transform herself from the image of the crying woman, or La Llorona, to that of the empowered, shouting woman—La Gritona, the name of the local creek."

Reception

With the publication of *Woman Hollering Creek and Other Stories* by Random House, Cisneros achieved national fame. For the first time, a Chicana writer's book was published by a mainstream press. As a result, many people read the book, and most reacted favorably, agreeing with reviewer Sheila Benson of the *Los Angeles Times* that the author was "a securely grounded woman, hollering in ringing tones, for all the world to hear," and with reviewer Marcia Tager of *Library Journal* that Cisneros "writes with humor and love about people she knows intimately." However, not all critics were thrilled with the book. For example, Miguel Sanchez Gracia described the title story as a "masterpiece of derogatory terms against Hispanic immigrants" and felt that Cisneros belittled and slandered Latinos. However, overall, the book was positively received and won several awards, including the PEN Center West Award for Best Fiction of 1991, the Lannan Foundation Literary Award for Fiction, and the Ansfield-Wolf Book Award for excellence in literature of diversity.

Critic Ellen McCracken claims that "the book established Cisneros as one of the foremost talents in contemporary American fiction. With innovative technical experiments in voice, narration, and themes, the twenty-two stories aesthetically reconfigure Latino ethnicity for various sectors of the reading public that differ in ethnicity, gender, age, and income." McCracken concludes that "[t]he book's wide appeal results both from the contemporary interest in multiculturalism and from Cisneros's postmodern narrative style with its multiple points of entry for diverse readers." Today, readers continue to praise the collection, finding it an important work that tells the stories of the lives of women who have not traditionally seemed important.

POETRY

CISNEROS FINDS POETRY A HIGHLY personal form of writing, "a little periscope that goes inside my psyche . . . [which] has nothing to do with publishing." In spite of her beliefs that her poems are too personal to publish, Cisneros's first publication was a short book of poetry called *Bad Boys*, printed in 1980. Since then Cisneros has published two books of poetry, *My Wicked Wicked Ways* in 1987 and *Loose Woman* in 1994.

My Wicked Wicked Ways consists of sixty poems, including the seven poems from *Bad Boys,* that Cisneros composed primarily when she was a graduate student in Iowa. The book is "a collection of poetry celebrating the 'bad girl' with her 'lopsided symmetry of sin and virtue.'" *Loose Woman*, a highly personal book of poems celebrating Cisneros's freedom from repressive ideas about how a woman should behave, deals with love and desire, showing the experiences of a passionate woman. It is filled with earthy language, vivid comparisons, and mature themes. In general, Cisneros's poems are emotional pieces that are not very complicated works: the diction consists of common words, the allusions and images are easy

My Wicked Wicked Ways

SANDRA CISNEROS

POEMS

Though best known for her prose, Sandra Cisneros has published
three books of poetry, many of which celebrate the "bad girl" in her.

to understand, and the meanings are usually apparent on a first reading.

Among the poems in Cisneros's books are "Abuelito Who," "Good Hot Dogs," "His Story," and "Peaches—Six in a Tin Bowl, Sarajevo" from *My Wicked Wicked Ways* and "Arturito the Amazing Baby Olmec Who Is Mine by Way of Water" and "Once Again I Prove the Theory of Relativity" from *Loose Woman*.

"Abuelito Who"

"Abuelito Who" reveals a child's feelings about her dying grandfather, in Spanish called Abuelito, by using two time frames: the first part of the poem, lines 1–15, is filled with memories she has of her grandfather when he was alive; the second part, lines 16–23, depicts the way she feels about those recollections. The child describes her grandfather as a man who plays a love game with her by asking "who loves him," while letting her know that he loves her, telling her in both Spanish and English that she is "my diamond" and "my sky."

Sadly, the sick man can no longer "come out to play" with her. Dying and "tired," he needs to be left alone, telling his granddaughter to "shut the door" so he can sleep "in his little room all night and day." Then he disappears from her sight. She says either he "doesn't live here anymore" or he "is hiding underneath the bed." Even though she can no longer see his physical body, he has not left her. He not only "talks to me inside my head," but he has become a part of the natural world that surrounds her, and he still plays a love game with her by asking, "who loves him / who loves him who?"

To show the close relationship between the grandfather and the child, Cisneros structures the twenty-three-line poem with a frame by using similar words at the beginning and the end—"who loves him"—and parallel images of rain. The living grandfather "throws coins like rain," while the spiritual entity actually is "the rain on the roof that falls like coins."

Cisneros achieves a type of rhythm by using a series of twelve dependent clauses introduced by the relative pronouns "who" and "whose" and a sequence of eleven short phrases that begin with verbs.

The poem is rich with similes and metaphors. Cisneros remembers her grandfather as "dough and feathers," painting a picture of a man with a body as soft as bread dough or feather pillows. As he lies sick in his bed, he is "a watch and glass of water," a man who keeps a close eye on the time so he knows when he needs to take his pills, which he washes down with water. His laughter is combined with a hacking cough, making it sound "like the letter k." His bedroom, reeking with the smell of sickness that is apparent as soon as a person opens the door, is "a doorknob tied to a sour stick." Even after her grandfather is dead, she remembers him as "blankets and spoons and big brown shoes," an old, worn-out, and possibly smelly, bedridden man who takes spoonfuls of medicine. By the end of the poem, he "is the rain on the roof," a part of nature.

Unlike many poems written about the death of a loved one, Cisneros's poem is not sentimental or extremely sad. Rather, it is a realistic picture of the sickness and death of a loved grandfather who continues to love and be near his granddaughter after he dies.

"Good Hot Dogs"

This delightful poem uses all of the five senses to help readers participate in the experience of enjoying delectable hot dogs. Cisneros starts with the sense of smell, calling the hot dog store a place "That smelled like steam." Then she zeroes in on the hotdogs by using the sense of sight, making readers see "Everything on the hot dogs / Except pickle lily"—the "Yellow mustard and onions / And french fries piled on top." Next she makes readers feel the "hot" sandwiches wrapped in wax paper. After that she turns to the sense of taste, as the children quickly eat the hot dogs, devouring "even / The little burnt tips / Of french fries," leaving nothing "But salt and poppy seeds." To show the happiness of the children, Cisneros uses the sense of sound ("You humming") and the kinesthetic sense of motion ("And me swinging my legs").

To show the children's impatience to get out of school so they can run to the store to buy great hot dogs, Cisneros makes her poem race along by using short words and short lines. She also uses a technique known as "enjambment": placing words in two separate lines that normally go together such as "wax" and "Paper," and "eat" and "Fast," to make readers "race to the next line without a breath."

The entire poem presents a picture of the happiness and contentment that two children find by enjoying the simple things of life.

"His Story"

This autobiographical poem, according to teacher Carol Jago, is a description of Cisneros's "status in a Mexican-American

family as seen from her father's point of view." Because she is an only daughter in a family with six sons, she says she is bound to have "An unlucky fate." She describes her father's "sorrow" because she was "born under a crooked star" and was, therefore, going to turn out to be a bad woman like the five women he describes. He begins by telling her that becoming a bad woman is a "family trait," as seen in three wicked women in her family: her beautiful great-aunt who "lived mistress. / Died solitary," her cousin who "ran off with the colonel" and "the army payroll," and her great-grandmother "who died a death of voodoo."

He then tells her that her name, Sandra Cisneros, further confirms that she will turn out bad because he knows of two cursed women who share her name. One "was arrested for audacious crimes" after "disobeying fathers," and the other "was three times cursed a widow." In the final short lines, Cisneros reveals how she has fulfilled her father's prophecies by doing something her father feels is her downfall: she has left his home.

The poem not only reveals her father's point of view but also Cisneros's feelings. Because of her father's attitude toward her, she sees herself as an unwanted "only daughter / whom no one came for." She makes it clear that her father's attempts to control her by telling her about bad women have caused her to rebel in order to find freedom.

"His Story" is a sad reflection of a father/daughter relationship. The father's sorrow is that he feels his daughter has turned out to be bad since she has become independent. Her sorrow is that her father's overly protective attitude toward her has caused a rift between them.

"Peaches—Six in a Tin Bowl, Sarajevo"

The six peaches sitting in a tin bowl in Sarajevo are a metaphor for people who are involved in loving human relationships. In this reflective poem, Cisneros remembers a time of deep contentment when she and her loved one could touch each other and sleep peacefully together, like soft, fuzzy peaches touching one another in a bowl. Cisneros personifies the peaches, giving them human characteristics, as she pictures them as loving people who "hold one another" in their arms, "nudge one another" with their feet, and "sleep / with their dimpled head / on the other's."

"Arturito the Amazing Baby Olmec Who Is Mine by Way of Water"

This poem is Cisneros's tribute to her godson, Arturo Javier Cisneros Zamora, born February 8, 1993. The title reflects her closeness to the baby, as she calls him "Arturito," a pet way of saying his given name, Arturo. Not only is he an "Amazing Baby," but he is also an "Olmec," referring to a prehistoric people that lived on the coast of Veracruz. She proudly claims him as her own by the waters of baptism because she is his godmother, even though she supposedly is "the aunt who dislikes kids and Catholics."

After relating that Arturito is "a wonder, a splendor, a plunder," she becomes like a fairy godmother and bestows three wishes on him. She wishes him to be noble like the Mexican hero Zapata, "who guards / those weaker than himself"; to be wise like the Indian leader Mahatma Gandhi, who

"Arturito . . ."
is a tribute to
Cisneros's godson,
to whom she is
very close.

"knew power is not the fist, / he knew the power of the powerless"; and to be generous like saintly Mother Teresa, who understood that "wealth is giving / yourself away to others."

In this poem, Cisneros expresses her tender love, ardent pride, and fervent joy for her amazing godson.

"Once Again I Prove the Theory of Relativity"

Cisneros takes the title of this poem about lost love from Albert Einstein's theory of relativity, a complicated scientific theory that explains how time and space operate in the universe to cause a change in objects. Cisneros uses Einstein's words to reveal how the passage of time and the absence of her loved one have made her desire him more. Separated by time and space, the narrator writes about her passionate longings and her desires for his return.

The narrator, showing intense feelings for her beloved, absent lover, describes him as a type of god. In the first stanza, she uses exotic similes to express the elation she would feel if he would return, claiming she would "treat you / like a lost Matisse," a painting or sculpture made by the French artist Henri Matisse; "couch you like a Pasha," a high-ranking Turkish officer; do acrobatics "like a Taiwanese diva"; "bang cymbals like a Chinese opera"; and "roar like a Fellini [an Italian movie director] soundtrack." She concludes this stanza with a fun, down-to-earth comparison from a common nursery rhyme, asserting that she would "laugh like the little dog that / watched the cow jump over the moon."

After describing how she would act, the narrator reflects on her lover's beauty, which is like "the color inside an ear," "a conch shell," and "a Modigliani [an Italian painter and sculptor famous for his beautiful nudes] nude." By the end of the poem, she reveals that she knows her lover will leave her again, but since she has "savored you like an oyster," she will be able to write poems about him.

The poem is a beautiful description that proves that absence and time make the heart grow fonder.

Reception

Although Cisneros's books of poetry have never reached the critical or popular acclaim of her works of fiction, they, especially *Loose Woman*, are admired by a number of readers and critics. The *Detroit Free Press* reviewer asserts that in this book, "Readers are drawn to her magnetic images, her liberal use of Spanish words and expressions, and her blending of poetry and prose," while a *Poets and Writers* critic claims that Cisneros's "poetry intoxicates." Fellow authors

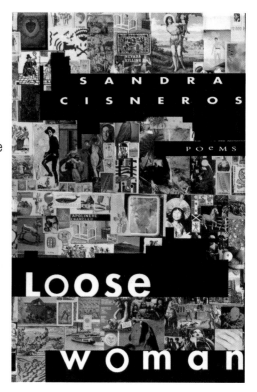

The poems in *Loose Woman* have won praise for their magnetic images, earthy humor, and passion.

have lavished praise on *Loose Woman*. Friend and writer Joy Harjo professed to "love these poems," which are "accomplished" and "won't disappoint"; author Ana Castillo wrote that "Sandra Cisneros has penned poetry of utterly divine language and imagery"; writer Cristina Garcia found *Loose Woman* "[f]ierce, intoxicating, hilarious"; and author Jessica Hagedorn proclaimed that "Sandra Cisneros's *Loose Woman* is a hothouse feast of word-play, divine love, earthy humor, mariachi yearnings, and powerhouse passion."

A number of readers appreciate both of Cisneros's books of poetry, finding, as Cisneros herself put it, that *My Wicked Wicked Ways* is "like classical music," while *Loose Woman* "is more like jazz."

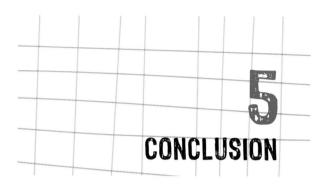

CONCLUSION

SANDRA CISNEROS MADE HER MARK in the literary world in 1984 with the publication of *The House on Mango Street*, a novel she had begun writing as a reaction against the types of works promoted by her graduate school professors. Frustrated and angry that all the books they read in school were about mainstream Americans, Cisneros determined to write something different, something that would relate to the lives of poor Latinos. Today, *Mango Street* is praised by both minority and mainstream Americans and hailed as a masterpiece.

It took some time for the book to be widely accepted. In the 1980s and 1990s, it was at the forefront of university discussions about diversity and inclusiveness as members of academia fought about whether the literary canon should continue to consist exclusively of traditional Western civilization works or whether it should include multicultural writings such as *The House on Mango Street*. Traditionalists lost the battle, and by the late 1990s, multicultural writings were part of most college English department curriculums. Cisneros was one of the major Chicana representatives, a

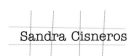

position she earned not only because of *The House on Mango Street* but also because of her subsequent works, particularly her collection of short stories, *Woman Hollering Creek and Other Stories*. In 1998, six of Cisneros's stories were included in the *Norton Anthology of American Literature*, a major victory for a minority writer. More than a decade later, her stories are often found in anthologies of American and women's literature used in university classrooms.

However, not all of Cisneros's works have found their way into multicultural courses. Basically, her stories told from a child's point of view have been adopted, while her works containing mature subject matter—her adult short stories found in *Woman Hollering Creek*, her collections of erotic poems, and her novel *Caramelo*—have been largely excluded from high school classrooms, ignored in academia, omitted in college anthologies, and often overlooked by critics because of their explicit sexual content or their angry, disenchanted narrators who are not seen as positive role models. Cisneros's coming-of-age stories remain her most popular writings.

Although her works are not all equally well known, Cisneros has become a famous Latina writer during the past twenty-five years as Americans have recognized more and more writers of diversity. This national acceptance of multicultural writers can be seen by Cisneros's publication history. She has been able to move from being published by small presses devoted to printing works solely by Latino/a writers to being published by mainstream companies. In 1980, her first book, *Bad Boys*, was printed by Mango Press in the Chicano Chapbook series, while her second work, *The*

House on Mango Street, was published by Arte Público Press, a Latino/a press in Houston, in 1984. Although the novel received high praise as a work by a Chicana writer, Cisneros still did not break into mainstream America; therefore, in 1987, *My Wicked Wicked Ways* was published by another independent publishing house, Third Woman Press.

Things changed for Cisneros in the early 1990s, a time that publisher Joseph Barbato of *Publishers Weekly* identifies as "a period of transition for Latino writers." He explains that with the country's "movement for multicultural literacy," many Latino writers, including Cisneros, no longer needed to publish in small, ethnic companies, because large, national publishing houses were now interested in their works. Cisneros was "the first Chicana writing about Chicano themes to publish a book with a mainstream press," Random House, which published her collection of twenty-two short stories, *Woman Hollering Creek*, in 1991 and reissued *The House on Mango Street* in 1991 and *My Wicked Wicked Ways* in 1992. Two years later, Knopf, a division of Random House, published *Loose Woman* and *Hairs/Pelitos*. When Cisneros completed *Caramelo* in 2002, Knopf published it, and remained her publisher when *Have You Seen Marie?* was released in 2012. Thus, all of Cisneros's works, with the exception of *Bad Boys*, have been published by mainstream presses, giving Cisneros a large reading audience in mainstream America.

She also has a broad Spanish-speaking reading public because Vintage Books, another division of Random House, issued Spanish translations of Cisneros's fiction, reissuing *The House on Mango Street* in 1995, *Woman Hollering Creek*

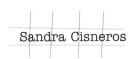
in 1996, and *Caramelo* in 2002. In addition, many of Cisneros's books have been translated into other languages.

Consequently, her works continue to be read and loved by a wide range of audiences, with *The House on Mango Street* remaining her most dearly loved work. In 2009, Cisneros reissued her book about Esperanza and completed a successful multi city tour celebrating its twenty-fifth year of publication. Today Cisneros, one of the most famous and popular of the minority writers in America, is also internationally acclaimed, held in high esteem by a number of academics, critics, publishers, and the general reading public.

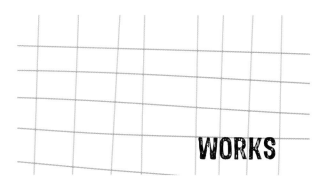

WORKS

1980 *Bad Boys*; reprinted in *My Wicked Wicked Ways*

1984 *The House on Mango Street*, reissued by Vintage Books, 1991
Spanish version: *La Casa en Mango Street*, 1995

1987 *My Wicked Wicked Ways*, reissued by Random House, 1992

1991 *Woman Hollering Creek and Other Stories*
Spanish version: *El Arroyo de la Llorona y Otros Cuentes*, 1996

1994 *Loose Woman*

1994 *Hairs/Pelitos*

2002 *Caramelo*
Spanish version: Caramelo, or Puro Cuento, 2002

2003 *Vintage Cisneros*

2012 *Have You Seen Marie?*

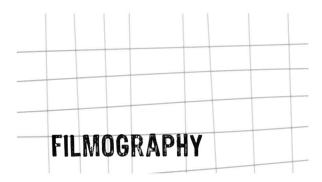

FILMOGRAPHY

Film

Conversations with Intellectuals about Selena. Dir. Lourdes Portillo. Xochitl Productions. 1999.

The Latino List. Dir. Timothy Greenfield-Sanders. Perfect Day Films. 2010.

Woman Hollering Creek. Dir. Joy Lusco Kecken and Scott Kecken. The Film Foundry. 2004.

Television

Invitations to World Literature. Dir. Joshua Seftel. TV documentary; Annenberg Media/Seftel Productions. 2010.

Literary Visions. Dir. William Scott Bealmear and Scott Hilton Davis. TV documentary; Annenberg/CPB Project. 1992.

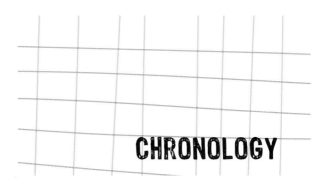

CHRONOLOGY

1954

Sandra Cisneros is born December 20 in Chicago to Alfredo Cisneros Del Moral and Elvira Cordero Anguiano Cisneros, their third child and only living daughter.

1959

Cisneros begins elementary school, first attending public school and later Catholic elementary schools, including St. Callistus and St. Aloysius.

1966

Cisneros's parents buy their first house, located in the Humboldt Park area of Chicago.

1968

Cisneros begins Josephinum High School, a Catholic all-girls school.

1972

Cisneros graduates from high school in the spring and enters Loyola University in Chicago in the fall.

1976

Cisneros graduates from Loyola with a B.A. in English in the spring and enters the University of Iowa Writers' Workshop MFA program in Creative Writing in the fall.

1978

Cisneros writes sketches for *The House on Mango Street*, completes a master's thesis called "My Wicked Wicked Ways," and receives an MFA in Creative Writing from the University of Iowa.

1978–1980

Cisneros teaches at Latino Youth Alternative High School in south Chicago. Her poetry is included in the Chicago Transit Authority's poetry project.

1980

Bad Boys, a chapbook (a short collection of poetry), is published by Mango Press.

1980–1982

Cisneros works as a counselor-recruiter for Loyola University.

1982

Cisneros receives her first National Endowment for the Arts Fellowship. In the summer she goes to Provincetown, Massachusetts, to work on *The House on Mango Street*; in the fall she travels to Greece, where she completes the novel.

1983

Cisneros serves as artist-in-residence at Michael Karolyi Artist's Foundation in Venice, Italy. She spends the summer in Sarajevo, Yugoslavia (now Bosnia), where she meets life-long friend Jasna Karaula. Cisneros works on revisions of *The House on Mango Street*.

1984

Cisneros returns to the United States. *The House on Mango Street* is published by Arte Público Press to rave reviews. Cisneros serves as the arts administrator of Guadalupe Cultural Arts Center in San Antonio, Texas. She is awarded an Illinois Artists Grant and the Texas Institute of Letters Dobie-Paisano Fellowship.

1985

The House on Mango Street wins the Before Columbus Foundation's American Book Award.

1986

Cisneros receives the Chicano Short Story Award from the University of Arizona.

1987

My Wicked Wicked Ways, a collection of sixty poems, is published by Third Woman Press.

1987–1988

Cisneros serves as a visiting lecturer at California State University, Chico.

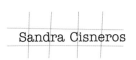

1988
Cisneros receives her second National Endowment for the Arts Fellowship. She contacts Susan Bergholz, a literary agent, who sells *Woman Hollering Creek and Other Stories* to Random House and *The House on Mango Street* to Vintage Books, a division of Random House. Cisneros receives the Roberta Holloway Lectureship at the University of California, Berkeley.

1989
Cisneros's father, Alfredo Cisneros, suffers a stroke.

1990
Cisneros serves as a guest professor at the University of California, Irvine, and the University of Michigan, Ann Arbor.

1991
Woman Hollering Creek and Other Stories, a collection of twenty-two short stories, is published by Random House; it is awarded the PEN Center West Award for Best Fiction of 1991 and the Lannan Foundation Literary Award for Fiction. Vintage Books reissues *The House on Mango Street*. Cisneros serves as a guest professor at the University of New Mexico, Albuquerque. She buys her first home, in the King William Historic District of San Antonio.

1992
Random House reissues *My Wicked Wicked Ways* and gives Cisneros advance payments for a new novel, *Caramelo*, and a new collection of poetry, *Loose Woman*. Cisneros travels to

Mexico with other Latino writers to introduce their works to Mexican and other Latin American readers.

1993

Cisneros becomes a peace activist in response to the war in Bosnia. She wins the Ansfield-Wolf Book Award for excellence in literature of diversity for *Woman Hollering Creek and Other Stories*. Cisneros is awarded an honorary Doctor of Letters degree from the State University of New York, Purchase.

1994

Loose Woman, a collection of poetry, and *Hairs/Pelitos*, a children's book, are published by Knopf, a division of Random House.

1995

Cisneros receives a MacArthur Foundation "genius grant." She hosts the Macondo Writing Workshop, which later becomes the Macondo Foundation. The Spanish translation of *The House on Mango Street* is published by Random House. Alfredo Cisneros has quadruple bypass surgery.

1996

Cisneros returns to Chicago to help care for her father, who is diagnosed with terminal cancer. The Spanish translation of *Woman Hollering Creek* is published.

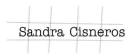

1997

Alfredo Cisneros dies on February 12. Cisneros paints her house purple, causing controversy in San Antonio. She helps initiate Los MacArturos.

1998

Cisneros is honored with a lifetime achievement award from the Mexican Fine Arts Center Museum, Chicago.

2000

Cisneros works to end capital punishment. She establishes the Alfredo Cisneros Del Moral Foundation.

2002

Caramelo, a novel, is published in English and Spanish by Knopf in October; it is selected as Notable Book of the Year by the *New York Times*, the *Los Angeles Times*, the *San Francisco Chronicle*, the *Chicago Tribune*, and the *Seattle Times*. Cisneros receives an honorary Doctor of Humane Letters degree from Loyola University, Chicago.

2003

Cisneros continues community work as a fund-raiser and adviser to community organizations. She is awarded the Texas Medal of the Arts. *Vintage Cisneros* is published.

2005

Caramelo is awarded the Premio Napoli; it is short-listed for the Dublin International IMPAC Award and nominated for the Orange Prize in England.

2006

Cisneros founds and becomes president of the Macondo Foundation. The University of Michigan at Ann Arbor awards Cisneros a King-Chávez-Parks Visiting Professor Award, and she is the keynote speaker at the university during Hispanic Heritage Month.

2007

Cisneros hosts a reunion of Los MacArturos in San Antonio on October 4–6. Her mother, Elvira Cordero Cisneros, dies on November 1.

2008

Cisneros establishes the Elvira Cordero Cisneros Award for the Macondo Foundation.

2009

Cisneros travels to twenty cities in the United States to celebrate the twenty-fifth anniversary of the publication of *The House on Mango Street*. She continues to work on a collection of fiction titled *Infinito*, a children's book called *Bravo, Bruno*, and a book about writing titled *Working in My Pajamas*.

2012

Have You Seen Marie?, a picture book for adults illustrated by Ester Hernandez, is published by Knopf in October.

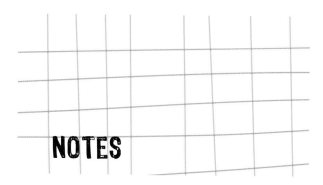

NOTES

Throughout the text, all references to Sandra Cisneros's works refer to the following editions of her works:

Caramelo, New York: Vintage Books, 2002.
The House on Mango Street, New York: Vintage Contemporaries, 2009.
Loose Woman, New York: Vintage Books, 1994.
My Wicked Wicked Ways, Berkeley: Third Woman Press, 1987.
Woman Hollering Creek and Other Stories, New York: Vintage Contemporaries, 1992.

Chapter One

p. 9, "Latinos" and "Latinas . . ." Virginia Brackett, *A Home in the Heart: The Story of Sandra Cisneros*, Greensboro, NC: Morgan Reynolds, 2005, 18.

p. 9, "erases the indigenous and African . . ." Ruth Behar, "Talking in Our Pajamas: A Conversation With Sandra Cisneros on Finding Your Voice, Fear of Highways, Tacos, Travel, and the Need for Peace in the World," *Michigan Quarterly Review* 47, no. 3, Summer 2008, 412.

pp. 9–10, "spent that first year gambling . . ." Feroza Jussawalla and Reed Way Dasenbrock, *Interviews With Writers of the Post-Colonial*

World, Jackson, MS: University Press of Mississippi, 1992, 297.

p. 10, "he ran away . . ." Jussawalla and Dasenbrock, *Interviews With Writers*, 297.

p. 10, "picked him up as . . ." Caryn Mirriam-Goldberg, *Sandra Cisneros: Latina Writer and Activist*, Springfield, NJ: Enslow Press, 1998, 14.

p. 10, "to ask the Puerto Ricans . . ." Sandra Cisneros, "Poem as Preface," *New York Times Book Review*, September 6, 1992, 1.

p. 10, "Well, I've heard there's . . ." Adria Bernardi, "Latino Voice," *Chicago Tribune,* August 4, 1991, K6.

p. 10, "simple and much more . . ." Wolfgang Binder, ed., *Partial Autobiographies: Interviews with Twenty Chicano Poets*, Erlangen, Germany: Palm & Enke, 1985, 54.

p. 10, "steal your chickens . . ." Jussawalla and Dasenbrock, *Interviews With Writers*, 297.

p. 12, "settling in Flagstaff . . ." "Elvira 'Vera' Cisneros: Mother of Sandra Cisneros," Obituary. www.sandracisneros.com/2007-11-01_elviracisneros.php (accessed June 13, 2011).

p. 12, "returned like the tides." Binder, *Partial Autobiographies*, 55.

p. 12, "the only constant . . ." Sandra Cisneros, "Ghosts and Voices: Writing from Obsession," *Americas Review* 15, no. 1, Spring 1987, 69.

p. 12, "almost like a foreigner" because "in some sense" . . ." Pilar E. Rodriguez Aranda, "On the Solitary Fate of Being Mexican, Female, Wicked and Thirty-three: An Interview with Sandra Cisneros," *Americas Review* 19, no. 1, Spring 1990, 66.

pp. 12–13, "in Mexico, where she looked . . ." Mirriam-Goldberg, *Sandra Cisneros*, 2.

p. 13, "small," "run-down" apartments "infested . . ." Mirriam-Goldberg, *Sandra Cisneros*, 17–18.

p. 13, "terrified" of "[m]ice . . ." Behar, "Talking in Our Pajamas," 419.

p. 13, "to me mice are all my poverty . . ." Sheila Benson, "From the Barrio to the Brownstone," *Los Angeles Times*, May 7, 1991, F1.

p. 13, "on the living room couch . . ." Aranda, "On the Solitary Fate," 66.

p. 13, "excluded me . . ." and "had their own . . ." Cisneros, "Ghosts," 69.

p. 13, "I have seven sons . . ." Sandra Cisneros, "Only Daughter," *Glamour*, November 1990, 256.

p. 13, "Not seven sons. . . ." Cisneros, "Only Daughter," 256.

p. 14, "his favorite." Sandra Cisneros, "Introduction: A House of My Own," *The House on Mango Street*, New York: Vintage Contemporaries, 2009, xii.

p. 14, "seven fathers . . ." Aranda, "On the Solitary Fate," 68.

p. 14, "pampered only daughter . . ." Bob Edwards, "Sandra Cisneros Looks Back," Interview, *PRI's Bob Edwards Weekend*, April 5, 2009, www.pri.org/arts-entertainment/books/sandra-cisneros-bob-edwards.html (accessed June 13, 2011).

p. 14, "that part of the reason . . ." Martha Satz, "Returning to One's House: An Interview with Sandra Cisneros," *Southwest Review* 82, no. 2, Spring 1997, par. 138.

p. 14, "I guess as Mexican daughters . . ." Aranda, "On the Solitary Fate," 73.

p. 15, "a freethinker, very bright . . ." Bridget Kevane and Juanita Heredia, "A Home in the Heart: An Interview with Sandra Cisneros," *Latina Self-Portraits: Interviews with Contemporary Women Writers*, Albuquerque: University of New Mexico Press, 2000, 55.

p. 15, "Puccini opera" and "a dinner . . ." Sandra Cisneros, "Notes to a Young(er) Writer," *Americas Review* 15, no. 1, Spring 1987, 75.

p. 15, "a prisoner of war. . . ." Behar, "Talking in Our Pajamas," 422.

p. 15, "didn't want me to inherit . . ." Cisneros, "Notes," 75.

p. 15, "herded her kids . . ." Cisneros, "Introduction," xiv.

p. 15, "if it weren't for her . . ." Satz, "Returning to One's Home," par. 32.

p. 15, "Because of my mother . . ." Robin Ganz, "Sandra Cisneros: Border Crossings and Beyond," *MELUS* 19, no. 1, Spring 1994, 22.

p. 15, "was always creating . . ." Kevane and Heredia, "A Home," 47.

p. 17, "I'd been writing stories . . ." Cisneros, "Introduction," xv.

p. 17, "always supported the daughter's . . ." Cisneros, "Introduction," xiv.

p. 17, "Good lucky . . ." Cisneros, "Introduction," xiv.

p. 17, "were so valuable . . ." Cisneros, "Ghosts," 71.

p. 17, "keeper of swans . . ." and "ridiculous, ugly . . ." Cisneros, "Ghosts," 71.

p. 17, *The Little House* the house . . ." Cisneros, "Ghosts," 71.

p. 17, "That was the plan . . ." Cisneros, "Ghosts," 71.

p. 18, "small, ugly two-story . . ." Mirriam-Goldberg, *Sandra Cisneros*, 26.

p. 18, "a narrow closet . . ." and "long as a coffin . . ." Sandra Cisneros, "Guadalupe: The Sex Goddess," *Ms.*, July–August 1996, 44.

p. 18, "big, hulky, and authoritarian . . ." Brackett, *A Home in the Heart*, 23.

p. 18, "were majestic at making . . ." Jim Sagel, "Sandra Cisneros," Interview, *Publishers Weekly* 238, no. 15, March 29, 1991, 74.

p. 18, "[g]irls, and especially poor . . ." Mirriam-Goldberg, *Sandra Cisneros*, 26.

p. 19, "very racist . . ." and "the Italian kids . . ." Mirriam-Goldberg, *Sandra Cisneros*, 26.

p. 19, "[t]hey recognized that I . . ." Quoted in Mirriam-Goldberg, *Sandra Cisneros*, 28.

p. 19, "I would have thrown myself . . ." Cisneros, "Guadalupe," 44.

p. 19, "filled with pleas . . ." and "a few catchy . . ." Binder, *Partial Autobiographies*, 63.

pp. 19–20, "daughters were meant . . ." Aranda, "On the Solitary Fate," 68.

p. 20, "I remember my father . . ." Cisneros, "Only Daughter," 256.

p. 20, "I'm lucky my father . . ." Cisneros, "Only Daughter," 256.

p. 21, "was deadly for me . . ." Edwards, "Sandra Cisneros Looks Back."

p. 21, "terribly cruel to her . . ." Quoted in Mirriam-Goldberg, *Sandra Cisneros*, 41.

p. 21, "[t]here was competition . . ." Mirriam-Goldberg, *Sandra Cisneros*, 41.

p. 21, "that nobody cared to hear . . ." and "very frightened and terrified . . ." Quoted in Mirriam-Goldberg, *Sandra Cisneros*, 41.

p. 22, "a prison . . ." Jussawalla and Dasenbrock, *Interviews With Writers*, 302.

p. 22, "It was not until . . ." Sagel, "Sandra Cisneros," 74.

p. 22, "third-floor flats . . ." Cisneros, "Ghosts," 70.

p. 22, *The House on Mango Street* was born . . ." Binder, *Partial Autobiographies*, 63.

p. 23, "would become [a] life-long . . ." Cisneros, "Introduction," xvi.

p. 23, "Now she summoned . . ." and "sons and daughters . . ." Cisneros, "Introduction," xii–xiii.

p. 24, "to be a weather girl . . ." Cisneros, "Introduction," xv.

p. 24, "there are so many other things . . ." Cisneros, "Introduction," xi.

p. 24, "to live a life . . ." Cisneros, "Introduction," xiv.

p. 25, "four pages long . . ." Cisneros, "Introduction," xv.

p. 25, "stand alone while also . . ." and "[y]ou would understand . . ." Jussawalla and Dasenbrock, *Interviews With Writers*, 298.

p. 25, "I've never seen a model . . ." Aranda, "On the Solitary Fate," 71.

p. 26, "federally funded press.. . ." Ilan Stavans, "Sandra Cisneros:

Form over Content," *The Essential Ilan Stavans*, New York: Routledge, 2000, 42–43.

p. 26, "[b]y the late eighties . . ." Stavans, "Sandra Cisneros," 43.

p. 26, "the main domestic . . ." Oscar Handlin, "History of the United States," *World Book Encyclopedia*, Chicago: World Book, 1986, 122.

p. 26, "drive for equality . . ." Handlin, "History," 124.

p. 26, "became a visible part . . ." Bridget Kevane and Juanita Heredia, "Introduction," *Latina Self-Portraits: Interviews with Contemporary Women Writers*, Albuquerque: University of New Mexico Press, 2000, 3.

p. 26, "racial and cultural . . ." Homer D. C. García, "Mexican Americans," *World Book Encyclopedia*, Chicago: World Book, 1986, 368b.

p. 28, "the Chicano, civil rights, Puerto Rican . . ." Kevane and Heredia, "Introduction," 3.

p. 28, "the most wonderful friend . . ." Sandra Cisneros, *Caramelo*, New York: Vintage, 2002, 444.

p. 28, "4 am on the day . . ." Brackett, *A Home in the Heart*, 46.

p. 29, "quite there . . ." Brackett, *A Home in the Heart*, 46.

p. 29, "being a wife" and "I washed . . . " Sandra Cisneros, "Who Wants Stories Now?" *New York Times*, March 14, 1993, section 3, 17.

p. 29, "poetic and very touching . . ." Mirriam-Goldberg, *Sandra Cisneros*, 60.

p. 30, "part of the early wave . . ." Quoted in Mireya Navarro, "Telling a Tale of Immigrants Whose Stories Go Untold," *New York Times*, November 12, 2002, E-1.

p. 30, "[f]or the first time . . ." Brackett, *A Home in the Heart*, 55.

p. 31, "a landscape that matches . . ." Jussawalla and Dasenbrock, *Interviews With Writers*, 291.

p. 31, "her waiter boyfriend . . ." Mirriam-Goldberg, *Sandra Cisneros*, 67; see also Sagel, "Sandra Cisneros," 75.

p. 31, "[l]eaving San Antonio . . ." Mirriam-Goldberg, *Sandra Cisneros*, 67.

p. 31, "marriage. It's like . . ." Satz, "Returning to One's House," par. 92.

p. 31, "exhausting, as exhausting . . ." Aranda, "On the Solitary Fate," 71–72.

p. 32, "my private time . . ." Aranda, "On the Solitary Fate," 77.

p. 32, "habitually arrived . . ." Mirriam-Goldberg, *Sandra Cisneros*, 68.

p. 32, "felt that she did not respect . . ." Brackett, *A Home in the Heart*, 59.

p. 32, "that students had to stop . . ." Bracket, *A Home in the Heart*, 59.

p. 32, "I thought I couldn't teach. . . ." Sagel, "Sandra Cisneros," 74.

p. 33, "sort of resistance fighter . . ." Carol Jago, *Sandra Cisneros in the Classroom: "Do not forget to reach,"* Urbana, IL: National Council of Teachers of English, 2002, 33–34.

p. 33, "Men complained that she . . ." Brackett, *A Home in the Heart*, 63.

p. 33, "And why can't a feminist . . ." Aranda, "On the Solitary Fate," 69.

p. 33, "no one seemed to care . . ." Satz, "Returning to One's House," par. 42.

p. 34, "a Manhattan literary agent . . ." Stavans, "Sandra Cisneros," 43.

p. 34, "diversity and the politics . . ." Stavans, "Sandra Cisneros," 43.

p. 34, "catalyzed the boom . . ." Ellen McCracken, "Sandra Cisneros (1954–)," *Latino and Latina Writers*, vol. 1, Alan West-Durán, ed., New York: Charles Scribner's Sons, 2004, 232.

p. 34, "key accomplishment. . . ." McCracken, "Sandra Cisneros (1954–)," 231.

pp. 33–34, "a spokesfigure for . . ." Stavans, "Sandra Cisneros," 43.

pp. 35–36, "a milestone in Cisneros's career . . ." Brackett, *A Home in the Heart*, 77–78.

p. 36, "Sometimes all I want to do . . ." Aranda, "On the Solitary Fate," 72.

p. 37, "Where can we get . . ." Cisneros, "Only Daughter," 256.

p. 37, "she was the only Chicana . . ." Brackett, *A Home in the Heart*, 82.

pp. 37–38, "when a bookstore owner. . . ." Mirriam-Goldberg, *Sandra Cisneros*, 86.

p. 38, "flagrantly erotic . . ." Kathy Lowry, "The Purple Passion of Sandra Cisneros," *Texas Monthly* 25, no.10, October 1997, 148.

pp. 38–39, "too dangerous to publish . . .," "vitriolic . . .," and "very adverse reaction . . ." Satz, "Returning to One's House," par. 38.

p. 39, "that arts should serve . . ." Cisneros, "Introduction," xvii.

p. 39, "genius grants . . ." Brackett, *A Home in the Heart,* 89.

p. 39, "wings that allowed . . ." Cisneros, *Caramelo*, 444.

p. 40, "peace of mind," and "kind of security," Satz, "Returning to One's House," pars. 86, 90.

p. 40, "Those who still had doubts . . ." Satz, "Returning to One's House," pars. 86, 88.

p. 40, "The best gift . . ." and "he understands the level . . ." Satz, "Returning to One's House," pars. 132, 130.

p. 40, "very dear and close . . ." Kevane and Heredia, "A Home," 53–54.

pp. 40–41, "had to take off . . ." Robert Birnbaum, "Interview: Sandra Cisneros: Author of *Caramelo* Talks with Robert Birnbaum," *Identity Theory, A Web-Based Magazine of Literature and Culture*, December 4, 2002, par. 43.

p. 41, "watched him dissolve . . ." Sandra Cisneros, "An Offering to the Power of Language," *Los Angeles Times*, October 26, 1997, M-1.

p. 41, "having a knife . . ." Kevane and Heredia, "A Home," 54.

p. 41, "a piece of my heart . . ." Sandra Cisneros, "The Genius of Creative Flexibility," *Los Angeles Times*, February 22, 1998, M-2.

p. 41, "inevitable loss . . ." and "inevitable gain . . ." Cisneros, "Offering," M-1.

p. 41, "the spirituality . . ." Cisneros, "Offering," M-1.

p. 41, "when you lose a loved one . . ." Cisneros, "Offering," M-1.

p. 41, "inspires me now . . ." and "kindness and generosity . . ." Cisneros, "Genius," M-2.

p. 41, "a Buddhist . . ." Navarro, "Telling a Tale of Immigrants," E-1.

p. 42, "religious icon . . ." and "the consolation of . . ." Leslie Petty, "The 'Dual'-ing Images of la Malinche and la Virgen de Guadalupe in Cisneros's *The House on Mango Street*," *MELUS* 25, no. 2, Summer 2000, 120.

p. 42, "a very powerful, sexual . . ." Satz, "Returning to One's House," par. 62.

p. 42, "that guidance and love . . ." Behar, "Talking in Our Pajamas," 413.

p. 42, "vivid, intense, in-your-face . . ." Lowry, "The Purple Passion," 148.

p. 42, "narrow minded . . ." Lowry, "The Purple Passion," 148.

p. 42, "retinue of ardent feminists . . ." Lowry, "The Purple Passion," 148.

p. 43, "in part to make . . ." Cisneros, "Genius," M-2.

p. 44, "I tried my very best . . ." Birnbaum, "Interview," par. 127.

p. 44, "a joyful, fizzy novel . . ." Valeria Sayers, "*Caramelo:* Traveling with Cousin Elvis," *New York Times Book Review*, September 29, 2002, 24.

p. 44, "together aesthetic nuances . . ." McCracken, "Sandra Cisneros (1954–)," 245.

p. 44, "[t]he novel marks Cisneros's . . ." McCracken, "Sandra Cisneros (1954–)," 245.

p. 45, "I usually meditate . . ." Behar, "Talking in Our Pajamas," 413–414.

p. 45, "writing in the language . . ." Behar, "Talking in Our Pajamas," 414.

pp. 45–46, "your enemy is seated . . ." Behar, "Talking in Our Pajamas," 415.

p. 46, "is very cinematic . . ." Birnbaum, "Interview," par. 107.

p. 46, "a little book . . ." Birnbaum, "Interview," par. 91.

pp. 46–47, "a book that's for me . . ." Birnbaum, "Interview," par. 101.

p. 47, "talked in public . . ." Behar, "Talking in Our Pajamas," 413.

p. 47, *Have You Seen Marie?*, http://www.sandracisneros.com/have_you_seen_marie.php

p. 47, "Mexican marigold . . ." Cisneros, "Introduction," xxv.

p. 47, "yappy dogs, kamikaze . . ." Cisneros, "Introduction," xxv.

Chapter Two

p. 52, "struggles between what she . . ." Maria Elena de Valdes, "In Search of Identity in Cisneros's *The House on Mango Street,*" *Canadian Review of American Studies* 23, no. 1, Fall 1992, par. 7.

p. 52, "the search for the real . . ." Dianne Klein, "Coming of Age in Novels by Rudolfo Anaya and Sandra Cisneros," *English Journal* 81, no. 5, September 1992, 26.

p. 55, "which route [she] didn't want . . ." Sandra Cisneros, "Introduction: A House of My Own," *The House on Mango Street.* New York: Vintage Contemporaries, 2009, xxiv.

p. 56, "tensions between belonging . . ." Jacqueline Doyle, "More Room of Her Own: Sandra Cisneros' *The House on Mango Street,*" *MELUS* 19, no. 4, Winter 1994, 20.

p. 57, "Neither her culture . . ." Anna Marie Sandoval, *Toward a Latina Feminism of the Americas*, Austin: University of Texas Press, 2008, 25.

p. 57, "act of resistance . . ." Sonia Saldívar-Hull, *Feminism on the*

Border: Chicana Gender Politics and Literature, Berkeley: University of California Press, 2000, 102.

p. 57, "speak for herself . . ." Doyle, "More Room of Her Own," 26–27.

p. 58, "has rewritten for herself . . ." Sandoval, *Toward a Latina Feminism*, 32.

p. 58, "both to accept . . ." Doyle, "More Room of Her Own," 21.

p. 59, "a subtle sequential order . . ." Valdes, "In Search of Identity," par. 11.

p. 59, "anticipated departure . . ." Valdes, "In Search of Identity," par. 11.

p. 60, "a vital and dynamic . . .", "the harsh socioeconomic . . .", and "her personal dreams . . ." Nicholas Sloboda, "A Home in the Heart: Sandra Cisneros's *The House on Mango Street*," *Aztlan* 22, no. 2, Fall 1997, 90.

p. 62, "With her protagonist exhibiting . . ." Sloboda, "A Home in the Heart," 105.

p. 62, "sexuality is doubly threatening . . ." Leslie Petty, "The 'Dual'-ing Images of la Malinche and la Virgen de Guadalupe in Cisneros's *The House on Mango Street*," *MELUS* 25, no. 2, Summer 2000, 127.

p. 63, "Sally gains material wealth . . ." Sloboda, "A Home in the Heart," 101.

p. 64, "a sign—at once real . . ." Sloboda, "A Home in the Heart," 92.

p. 67, "encounters with men . . ." Doyle, "More Room of Her Own," 17.

p. 67, "Like Cinderella, the women . . ." Michelle Scalise Sugiyama, "Of Woman Bondage: The Eroticism of Feet in *The House on Mango Street*," *Midwest Quarterly* 41, no. 1, Autumn 1999, 18–19.

p. 70, "to symbolize female sexuality . . ." Sugiyama, "Of Woman Bondage," 14.

p. 71, "the threatening nature . . ." Ellen McCracken, "Sandra

Cisneros' *The House on Mango Street*: Community-Oriented Introspection and the Demystification of Patriarchal Violence," *Breaking Boundaries: Latina Writing and Critical Readings*, Asunción Horno-Delgado et al., eds. Amherst: University of Massachusetts, 1989, 67.

p. 71, "The shoe motif . . ." Sugiyama, "Of Woman Bondage," 15.

p. 71, "Edenic innocence . . ." Doyle, "More Room of Her Own," 16.

p. 72, "images of constricting . . ." Doyle, "More Room of Her Own,"14.

p. 72, "the Mother Goose character . . ." Doyle, "More Room of Her Own," 14.

p. 72, "two lives to date . . ." Ellen McCracken, "Sandra Cisneros (1954–)," *Latino and Latina Writers*, vol. 1, Alan West-Durán, ed., New York: Charles Scribner's Sons, 2004, 237.

p. 73, "[a]lthough the book was not . . ." McCracken, "Sandra Cisneros (1954–)," 237.

p. 73, "circumstances surrounding. . . ." Felicia J. Cruz, "On the 'Simplicity' of Sandra Cisneros's *The House on Mango Street*," *Modern Fiction Studies* 47, no. 4, 2001, 910.

p. 73, "witnessed a revitalized interest. . . ." Alvina Quintana, *Home Girls: Chicana Literary Voices*, Philadelphia: Temple University Press, 1996, 54.

p. 73, "inscribed themselves . . ." Nicolás Kanellos, Introduction, *The Hispanic Literary Companion*, Nicolás Kanellos, ed. Detroit: Invisible Ink, 1997, xix.

p. 73, "the standout among . . ." Cruz, "On the 'Simplicity,'" 910.

p. 74, "appeal of *Mango Street* . . .": Cruz, "On the 'Simplicity,'" 910.

p. 74, "enjoyed by readers . . ." Carol Jago, *Sandra Cisneros in the Classroom: "Do not forget to reach,"* Urbana, IL: National Council of Teachers of English, 2002, 51.

p. 74, "its nonintellectual themes . . .": Cruz, "On the 'Simplicity,'" 915.

p. 74, "the book offers a window . . .": Jago, *Sandra Cisneros*, 51.

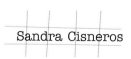

p. 74, "lavished enthusiastic praise . . .": Cruz, "On the 'Simplicity,'" 912.

Chapter Three

p. 75, "*Woman Hollering Creek* offers . . . " Harryette Mullen, "'A Silence Between Us Like a Language': The Untranslatability of Experience in Sandra Cisneros's *Woman Hollering Creek*," *MELUS* 21, no. 1, Summer 1996, 8.

p. 77, "as whole sections . . ." Jeff Thomson, "'What is Called Heaven': Identity in Sandra Cisneros's *Woman Hollering Creek*," *Studies in Short Fiction* 31, no. 3, Summer 1994, 416, 418.

p. 77, "girls seem secure . . . " Katherine Payant, "Borderland Themes in Sandra Cisneros's *Woman Hollering Creek*," *The Immigrant Experience in North American Literature: Carving Out a Niche*, Katherine B. Payant and Toby Rose, eds., Westport, Connecticut: Greenwood Press, 1999, 97.

p. 77, "toward situations where women . . ." Thomson, "'What is Called Heaven,'" 419.

p. 79, "the difficulty of maintaining . . ." Thomson, "'What is Called Heaven,'" 416–417.

p. 80, "stereotypes and enforced identity . . ." and "stereotypes that limit . . ." Thomson, "'What is Called Heaven,'" 417.

p. 80, "the films of Pedro Infante . . ." Thomson, "'What is Called Heaven,'" 417.

p. 82, "artificial feminine stereotypes . . ." Thomson, "'What is Called Heaven,'" 417.

p. 82, "seduced by the politics . . ." Barbara Brinson Curiel, "Sandra Cisneros, *Woman Hollering Creek and Other Stories*," *Reading U.S. Latina Writers: Remapping American Literature*, Alvina E. Quintana, ed., New York: Palgrave Macmillan, 2003, 54.

p. 82, "[t]hey realize the capitalist . . ." Curiel, "Sandra Cisneros," 54.

p. 82, "is both attacking . . ." Thomson, "'What is Called Heaven,'"

417.

p. 82, "that some children are . . ." Ellen McCracken, "Sandra Cisneros (1954–)," *Latino and Latina Writers*, vol. 1, Alan West-Durán, ed., New York: Charles Scribner's Sons, 2004, 241.

p. 83, "The reality of Seguin . . ." Payant, "Borderland Themes," 100.

p. 84, "juxtapos[ing] the heroines . . ." Jean Wyatt, "On Not Being La Malinche: Border Negotiations of Gender in Sandra Cisneros's 'Never Marry a Mexican' and 'Woman Hollering Creek,'" *Tulsa Studies in Women's Literature* 14, no. 2, Autumn 1995, 254.

p. 84, "that suffering is inherent . . ." Kristina K. Groover, "Reconstructing the Sacred: Latina Feminist Theology in Sandra Cisneros's *Woman Hollering Creek*," *English Language Notes* 44, no. 1, Spring 2006, 194.

p. 84, "for the submissions . . ." Wyatt, "On Not Being La Malinche," 255.

pp. 84–85, "lives in isolation . . ." and "characterizes Seguin . . ." Mary Pat Brady, "The Contrapuntal Geographies of *Woman Hollering Creek and Other Stories*," *American Literature* 71, no.1, March 1999, 140.

p. 86, "comes to realize . . ." Groover, "Reconstructing the Sacred," 194.

p. 86, "offer her different escape fantasies . . ." Mullen, "'A Silence Between Us," 11.

p. 87, "both the church and her community . . ." Groover, "Reconstructing the Sacred," 194.

p. 88, "[h]aving rejected the cultural message . . ." Groover, "Reconstructing the Sacred," 195.

p. 88, "appropriates for women . . ." Wyatt, "On Not Being La Malinche," 258.

p. 88, "she kills her three children . . ." Wyatt, "On Not Being La Malinche," 256.

p. 88, "killed the son . . ." and "Cortez wanted . . ." Wyatt, "On Not

Being La Malinche," 256.

pp. 88–89, "the Indians about to be slaughtered . . ." Wyatt, "On Not Being La Malinche," 256.

p. 89, "appears by the shore . . ." Wyatt, "On Not Being La Malinche," 256.

p. 89, "powerful and active . . ." Curiel, "Sandra Cisneros," 55.

p. 89, "a female figure whose cry . . ." Payant, "Borderland Themes," 102.

p. 89, "Cleófilas's laugh at the ending . . ." Payant, "Borderland Themes," 102.

p. 89, "that she must transform . . ." McCracken, "Sandra Cisneros (1954–)," 241.

p. 90, "a securely grounded woman . . ." Sheila Benson, "From the Barrio to the Brownstone," *Los Angeles Times*, May 7, 1991, F1.

p. 90, "writes with humor . . ." Marcia Tager, Review of "Cisneros, Sandra. *Woman Hollering Creek,*" *Library Journal*, April 1991, 149.

p. 90, "masterpiece of derogatory . . ." Quoted in Curiel, "Sandra Cisneros," 52.

p. 90, "the book established Cisneros . . ." McCracken, "Sandra Cisneros (1954–)," 240.

p. 90, "[t]he book's wide appeal . . ." McCracken, "Sandra Cisneros (1954–)," 240.

Chapter Four

p. 91, "a little periscope. . . ." Martha Satz, "Returning to One's House: An Interview with Sandra Cisneros," *Southwest Review* 82, no. 2, Spring 1997, par. 42.

p. 91, "a collection of poetry. . . ." Jim Sagel, "Sandra Cisneros," Interview, *Publishers Weekly* 238, no. 15, March 29, 1991, 74.

p. 95, "race to the next line . . ." Carol Jago, *Sandra Cisneros in the Classroom: "Do not forget to reach,"* Urbana, IL: National Council of Teachers of English, 2002, 30.

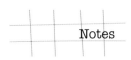

pp. 95–96, "status in a Mexican-American family . . .": Jago, *Sandra Cisneros*, 87.

p. 99, "Readers are drawn . . ." Quoted in Sandra Cisneros, *Loose Woman*, New York: Vintage, 1994, front pages.

p. 99, "poetry intoxicates . . ." Quoted in Cisneros, *Loose Woman*, front pages.

p. 100, "love these poems . . .", "accomplished", and "won't disappoint" Quoted in Cisneros, *Loose Woman*, front pages.

p. 100, "Sandra Cisneros has penned poetry . . ." Quoted in Cisneros, *Loose Woman*, front pages.

p. 100, "[f]ierce, intoxicating, hilarious . . ." Quoted in Cisneros, *Loose Woman*, front pages.

p. 100, "Sandra Cisneros's *Loose Woman* is . . ." Quoted in Cisneros, *Loose Woman*, front pages.

p. 100, "like classical music . . ." and "more like jazz . . ." Bridget Kevane and Juanita Heredia, "A Home in the Heart: An Interview with Sandra Cisneros," *Latina Self-Portraits: Interviews with Contemporary Women Writers,* Albuquerque: University of New Mexico Press, 2000, 48.

Conclusion

p. 101, "my own voice . . ." Sandra Cisneros, "Introduction," *The House on Mango Street*, New York: Alfred A. Knopf, 1994, xv.

p. 103, "a period of transition . . ." Joseph Barbato, "Latino Writers in the American Market," *Publishers Weekly* 238, no. 6, February 1, 1991, par. 8.

p. 103, "movement for multicultural . . ." Barbato, "Latino Writers," par. 21.

p. 103, "the first Chicana . . ." Ellen McCracken, "Sandra Cisneros (1954–)," *Latino and Latina Writers*, vol. 1, Alan West-Durán, ed., New York: Charles Scribner's Sons, 2004, 231.

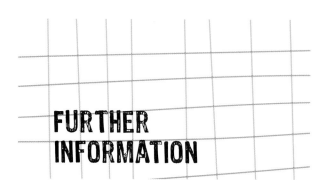

FURTHER INFORMATION

Brackett, Virginia. *A Home in the Heart: The Story of Sandra Cisneros.* Greensboro, NC: Morgan Reynolds, 2005.

Cisneros, Sandra. *Caramelo.* New York: Vintage Books, 2002.

———. *The House on Mango Street.* New York: Vintage Contemporaries, 1991.

———. *Loose Woman.* New York: Vintage Books, 1994.

———. *My Wicked Wicked Ways.* Berkeley: Third Woman Press, 1987.

———. *Vintage Cisneros.* New York: Vintage, 2004.

———. *Woman Hollering Creek and Other Stories.* New York: Vintage Contemporaries, 1991.

Jago, Carol. *Sandra Cisneros in the Classroom: "Do not forget to reach."* Urbana, IL: National Council of Teachers of English,

2002.

Kevane, Bridget, and Juanita Heredia. *Latina Self-Portraits: Interviews with Contemporary Women Writers*. Albuquerque: University of New Mexico Press, 2000.

Mirriam-Goldberg, Caryn. *Sandra Cisneros: Latina Writer and Activist*. Springfield, NJ: Enslow Press, 1998.

Saldívar-Hull, Sonia. *Feminism on the Border: Chicana Gender Politics and Literature*. Berkeley: University of California Press, 2000.

Sandoval, Anna Marie. *Toward a Latina Feminism of the Americas*. Austin: University of Texas Press, 2008.

Stavans, Ilan. *The Essential Ilan Stavans*. New York: Routledge, 2000.

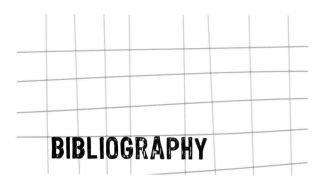

BIBLIOGRAPHY

Articles

Aranda, Pilar E. Rodriguez. "On the Solitary Fate of Being Mexican, Female, Wicked and Thirty-three: An Interview with Sandra Cisneros." *Americas Review* 19, no. 1 (Spring 1990): 64–80.

Barbato, Joseph. "Latino Writers in the American Market." *Publishers Weekly* 238, no. 6 (February 1, 1991): 17–21. *Expanded Academic ASAP.* Gale, July 10, 2009.

Behar, Ruth. "Talking in Our Pajamas: A Conversation With Sandra Cisneros on Finding Your Voice, Fear of Highways, Tacos, Travel, and the Need For Peace in the World." *Michigan Quarterly Review* 47, no. 3 (Summer 2008): 411–437.

Benson, Sheila. "From the Barrio to the Brownstone." *Los Angeles Times*, May 7, 1991, sec. F1.

Bernardi, Adria. "Latino Voice." *Chicago Tribune*, August 4, 1991, sec. K6.

Birnbaum, Robert. "Interview, Sandra Cisneros: Author of *Carmelo* Talks with Robert Birnbaum." *Identity Theory, A Web-Based Magazine of Literature and Culture* (December 4, 2002). www.identitytheory.com

Brady, Mary Pat. "The Contrapuntal Geographies of *Woman Hollering Creek and Other Stories.*" *American Literature* 71, no. 1 (March 1999): 117–150.

Cisneros, Sandra. "The Genius of Creative Flexibility." *Los Angeles Times,* February 22, 1998, sec. M-2.

———. "Ghosts and Voices: Writing from Obsession." *Americas Review* 15, no. 1 (Spring 1987): 69–73.

———. "Guadalupe: The Sex Goddess." *Ms.*, July–August 1996, 44.

———. "Notes to a Young(er) Writer." *Americas Review* 15, no. 1 (Spring 1987): 69–73.

———. "An Offering to the Power of Language." *Los Angeles Times,* October 26, 1997, sec. M-1.

———. "Only Daughter." *Glamour*, November 1990, 256–258.

———. "Poem as Preface." *New York Times Book Review,* September 6, 1992, 1.

———. "Who Wants Stories Now?" *New York Times,* March 14, 1993, sec. 4, 17.

Cruz, Felicia J. "On the 'Simplicity' of Sandra Cisneros's *The House on Mango Street.*" *Modern Fiction Studies* 47, no. 4 (2001): 910–946.

Doyle, Jacqueline. "More Room of Her Own: Sandra Cisneros' *The House on Mango Street.*" *MELUS* 19, no. 4 (Winter 1994): 6–35.

Edwards, Bob. "Sandra Cisneros Looks Back." Interview. *PRI's Bob Edwards Weekend,* April 5, 2009. www.pri.org

"Elvira 'Vera' Cisneros: Mother of Sandra Cisneros." Obituary. www.sandracisneros.com/2007-11-01_elvira_cisneros.php

Ganz, Robin. "Sandra Cisneros: Border Crossings and Beyond." *MELUS* 19, no. 1 (Spring 1994): 19–29.

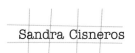

Groover, Kristina K. "Reconstructing the Sacred: Latina Feminist Theology in Sandra Cisneros's *Woman Hollering Creek.*" *English Language Notes* 44, no. 1 (Spring 2006): 191–197.

Klein, Dianne. "Coming of Age in Novels by Rudolfo Anaya and Sandra Cisneros." *English Journal* 81, no. 5 (September 1992): 21–26.

Lowry, Kathy. "The Purple Passion of Sandra Cisneros." *Texas Monthly* 25, no. 10 (October 1997): 148–150.

Mullen, Harryette. "'A Silence Between Us Like a Language': The Untranslatability of Experience in Sandra Cisneros's *Woman Hollering Creek.*" *MELUS* 21, no. 2 (Summer 1996): 3–20.

Navarro, Mireya. "Telling a Tale of Immigrants Whose Stories Go Untold." *New York Times,* November 12, 2002, sec. E-1.

Petty, Leslie. "The 'Dual'-ing Images of la Malinche and la Virgen de Guadalupe in Cisneros's *The House on Mango Street.*" *MELUS* 25, no. 2 (Summer 2000): 119–132.

Sagel, Jim. "Sandra Cisneros." Interview. *Publishers Weekly* 238, no. 15, March 29, 1991, 74–75. *Expanded Academic ASAP.* Gale, July 10, 2009.

Satz, Martha. "Returning to One's House: An Interview with Sandra Cisneros." *Southwest Review* 82, no. 2 (Spring 1997): 166–185. *Academic Search Elite.* EBSCO, (March 1, 2009).

Sayers, Valeria. "*Caramelo*: Traveling with Cousin Elvis." *New York Times Book Review*, September 29, 2002, 24.

Sloboda, Nicholas. "A Home in the Heart: Sandra Cisneros's *The House on Mango Street*." *Aztlan* 22, no. 2 (Fall 1997): 89–106.

Sugiyama, Michelle Scalise. "Of Woman Bondage: The Eroticism of Feet in *The House on Mango Street*." *Midwest Quarterly* 41, no. 1 (Autumn 1999): 9–20.

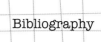
Tager, Marcia. Review of "Cisneros, Sandra. *Woman Hollering Creek.*" *Library Journal* (April 1991): 149.

Thomson, Jeff. "'What is Called Heaven': Identity in Sandra Cisneros's *Woman Hollering Creek.*" *Studies in Short Fiction* 31, no. 3 (Summer 1994): 415–424.

Valdes, Maria Elena de. "In Search of Identity in Cisneros's *The House on Mango Street.*" *Canadian Review of American Studies* 23, no. 1 (Fall 1992): 55–70. *Academic Search Elite.* EBSCO, (August 3, 2008).

Wyatt, Jean. "On Not Being La Malinche: Border Negotiations of Gender in Sandra Cisneros's 'Never Marry a Mexican' and 'Woman Hollering Creek.'" *Tulsa Studies in Women's Literature* 14, no. 2 (Autumn 1995): 243–271.

Books

Binder, Wolfgang, ed. *Partial Autobiographies: Interviews with Twenty Chicano Poets.* Erlangen, Germany: Palm & Enke, 1985.

Brackett, Virginia. *A Home in the Heart: The Story of Sandra Cisneros.* Greensboro, NC: Morgan Reynolds, 2005.

Cisneros, Sandra. *Caramelo.* New York: Vintage Books, 2002.

———. *Hairs/Pelitos.* New York: Apple Soup, 1994.

———. *Have You Seen Marie?* Ill. Ester Hernandez. New York: Knopf, 2012.

———. *The House on Mango Street.* New York: Vintage Contemporaries, 2009.

———. "Introduction: A House of My Own." *The House on Mango Street.* New York: Vintage Contemporaries, 2009. xi-xxvii.

———. *Loose Woman.* New York: Vintage Books, 1994.

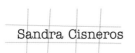

———. *My Wicked Wicked Ways*. Berkeley: Third Woman Press, 1987.

———. *Vintage Cisneros*. New York: Vintage, 2004.

———. *Woman Hollering Creek and Other Stories*. New York: Vintage Contemporaries, 1992.

Curiel, Barbara Brinson. "Sandra Cisneros, *Woman Hollering Creek and Other Stories*." *Reading U.S. Latina Writers: Remapping American Literature*. Edited by Alvina E. Quintana. New York: Palgrave Macmillan, 2003, 51–60.

García, Homer D. C. "Mexican Americans." *World Book Encyclopedia*. Chicago: World Book, 1986, 368–370.

Handlin, Oscar. "History of the United States." *World Book Encyclopedia*. Chicago: World Book, 1986, 86–126.

Jago, Carol. *Sandra Cisneros in the Classroom: "Do not forget to reach."* Urbana, IL: National Council of Teachers of English, 2002.

Jussawalla, Feroza, and Reed Way Dasenbrock. *Interviews With Writers of the Post-Colonial World*. Jackson: University Press of Mississippi, 1992.

Kanellos, Nicolás. Introduction. *The Hispanic Literary Companion*. Edited by Nicolás Kanellos. Detroit: Invisible Ink, 1997.

Kevane, Bridget, and Juanita Heredia. "A Home in the Heart: An Interview with Sandra Cisneros." *Latina Self-Portraits: Interviews with Contemporary Women Writers*. Albuquerque: University of New Mexico Press, 2000, 45–47.

———. "Introduction." *Latina Self-Portraits: Interviews with Contemporary Women Writers*. Albuquerque: University of New Mexico Press, 2000, 1–18.

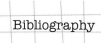
McCracken, Ellen. "Sandra Cisneros' *The House on Mango Street*: Community-Oriented Introspection and the Demystification of Patriarchal Violence." *Breaking Boundaries: Latina Writing and Critical Readings.* Edited by Asunción Horno-Delgado et al. Amherst: University of Massachusetts, 1989, 62–71.

———. "Sandra Cisneros (1954–)." *Latino and Latina Writers.* Vol. 1. Edited by Alan West-Durán. New York: Charles Scribner's Sons, 2004, 62–71.

Mirriam-Goldberg, Caryn. *Sandra Cisneros: Latina Writer and Activist.* Springfield, NJ: Enslow Press, 1998.

Olivares, Julián. "Sandra Cisneros' *The House on Mango Street* and the Poetics of Space." *Chicana Creativity and Criticism: Charting New Frontiers in American Literature.* Edited by Maria Herrera-Sobek and Helena Maria Viramontes. Houston, TX: Arte Público Press, 1988, 160–169.

Payant, Katherine. "Borderland Themes in Sandra Cisneros's *Woman Hollering Creek.*" *The Immigrant Experience in North American Literature: Carving Out a Niche.* Edited by Katherine B. Payant and Toby Rose. Westport, CT: Greenwood Press, 1999, 95–108.

Quintana, Alvina. *Home Girls: Chicana Literary Voices.* Philadelphia: Temple University Press, 1996.

Saldívar-Hull, Sonia. *Feminism on the Border: Chicana Gender Politics and Literature.* Berkeley: University of California Press, 2000.

Sandoval, Anna Marie. *Toward a Latina Feminism of the Americas.* Austin: University of Texas Press, 2008.

Stavans, Ilan. "Sandra Cisneros: Form over Content." *The Essential Ilan Stavans.* New York: Routledge, 2000, 41–46.

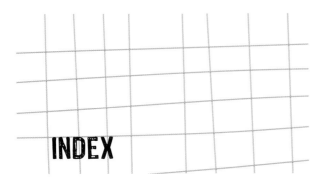

INDEX

Page numbers in **boldface** are photographs. Proper names of fictional characters are shown by (C).

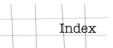

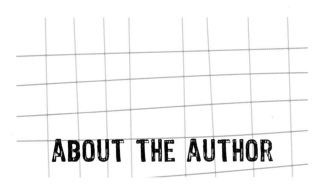

ABOUT THE AUTHOR

RAYCHEL HAUGRUD REIFF, a professor of English at the University of Wisconsin-Superior, has published many articles on literary topics and effective teaching techniques, as well as a number of books. Her most recent books for Cavendish Square are *William Golding: Lord of the Flies* and *Aldus Huxley: Brave New World*, in the Writers and Their Works series.